MIREH
MEMC

Recollections from a West Cumbrian community

Compiled and edited by Sue Donnelly
for Mirehouse Residents Group

First published in 2015
by
Mirehouse Residents Group
Registered Charity no 1148562. Company limited by guarantee 8197697

Front cover photograph by Roger Wynne.

ISBN No: 978-0-9933584-0-1

Printed and bound by:

The Firpress Group
Unit 5a, Buddle Road, Clay Flatts,
Workington, Cumbria CA14 3YD

Editor's Dedication

For Bridget, whose loyal friendship and true heart I shall miss deeply.
I know you would have enjoyed these narratives, Bridget,
if only time had been a little kinder to you.

Publisher's Dedication

This book is dedicated to current and past residents of Mirehouse
and members of the Mirehouse Residents Group who have all
contributed so much, over so many years, to making this a place
where we are proud to live.

Contents

Acknowledgements   7

Foreword   8

Introduction   9

Happy As Larks – *Jenny Doran*   11

Everyone Fitted In – *Laura Reed*   17

A Pocketful Of Fish – *Betty Armstrong*   20

A Hand On My Shoulder – *Sadie Nicholson*   24

Two Kinds Of Horses – *Betty Burney*   31

Flowing Like A Waterfall – *Moira Nesbitt*   37

Wild Flowers Everywhere – *Roger Wynne*   41

Tradesman's Entrance – *Janet Wynne*   44

My Link Road Lake (Poem) – *Jenny Doran*   49

The Calder Club (Poem) – *Jenny Doran*   50

Sink Or Swim – *Betty Wells*   51

It All Went In The Purse – *Kath McLean*   55

Vimto And A Straw – *Anne Chambers*   59

An Empty House On Greenbank – *Edith Dickinson*   63

Taking Root – *Alice Lindsay*   70

God's Country – *Berny Robson*   74

Maps   78

Acknowledgements

We are grateful to the following groups and organisations for providing the funding and support to enable the production of this book:

Mirehouse Residents Group members for their stories and personal photographs

Age UK West Cumbria Community Facilitators Project

Staff at Cumbria Records Office, Whitehaven

The Whitehaven News

Copeland Community Fund

Home Group

Cumbria County Council Archive Service

Copeland Borough Council

Mike Gregson

Alison Harker

Mirehouse Residents Group

Supported by **The National Lottery**® through the Heritage Lottery Fund

heritage lottery fund

Foreword

For many of us, our sense of personal identity is shaped, at least in part, by our experience of rootedness in place and community. For West Cumbrians, whose families may have been long established within a small geographical area, this feeling can be a particularly strong. This anthology contains a collection of oral histories contributed by some of the current and former residents of one small locality, the Mirehouse estate in South Whitehaven. The estate has a current population of approximately four and a half thousand and was built in the early 1950s to meet an increasing demand for housing as the nuclear industry grew in West Cumbria. It is characterised by having been built in two distinct halves, originally divided by a railway line. Each half became identifiable to locals by the respective bus route numbers that once served them, the 06 and the 09.

For the most part, the contributors to the anthology are drawn from the group of people who regularly participate in activities organised by the Mirehouse Residents Group, the publishers of this book. The fact that the majority of the narratives are from women reflects the current gender balance of those participants. Some of them were among the first residents to move into Mirehouse and the anthology contains recollections of their lives on the estate. But it also contains, in great part, accounts of their earlier years and how they came to be living in this area.

This is not a book of factual details, but a book of living histories, with all the colour, emotion and personal meaning that memory attaches to itself. As well as describing collective experiences, these narratives bring the contributors alive as individuals, with their own unique stories to tell alongside the ones they have shared. In carrying out the interviews for this book, I often felt I had been given a personal gift by the people involved, as they unfolded their lives for me. I hope as readers of this anthology you will enjoy a similar experience.

Sue Donnelly
Editor

Introduction

The idea for this book came about at a Mirehouse Residents Group coffee morning. I am employed by the group as their Coordinator, basically to get more residents involved in activities, attract funding and to engage with agencies to improve the area in general. Being a Workington lad, I was unaware of the history of Mirehouse and, although I had worked in the South Whitehaven area for some time, there was little written evidence to be found. So, over a coffee and a Kit Kat I started to chat. Without a doubt, the best feature of Mirehouse estate is the people that live within its boundaries and the warmth of their friendship. When I first started enquiring, the responses came thick and fast, along with many humorous stories which just had to be captured somewhere. With advice from the Heritage Lottery and their generous funding, we started along the road that is Mirehouse Memories, and the collation and production of this book. Our visits to the local archives were really exciting, from the discovery of the origins of the estate, Sellafield workers housing agreements with Copeland Borough Council for wider housing, through to stock transfer, and culminating in the discovery of a previous Valley Tenants and Residents Group in the fifties. While not exactly a definitive history of the estate, this is a history of the people, many now widows, that brought the area to life and gave it a soul. Mirehouse Residents Group and I thank all the contributors for their honesty, patience, time and for the memories they have so generously shared with us. We hope you enjoy reading the recollections as much as we did putting them together.

Keith Cartner
Mirehouse Residents Group

Happy as Larks

I was born in 1927 in the village of Blennerhasset. Dad took us once to show us the old house where we were born, all tumbled down now. I was a twin. The two doctors that looked after mam wanted us to be called after them, if we were boys. But they were William and Thomas, so we'd have had to be Wilhelmina and Thomasina! I used to say to my husband Billy, 'Just think, we could have been two Willies!'

Dad had got work at Whitehaven Brick and Tile Company, so that's why the family came here. We first lived in Fox Lane in Whitehaven, behind Dixons shop, then, when I was three or four, we went to Woodhouse. I often wonder why I was allowed to live and my twin, Lily, was took. She was eighteen months old, walking, talking when gastroenteritis killed her. I have just one photo of her, us together in the pram. I had an older sister, Violet, was killed when she came off the back of a bike. One brother was dead born. I never really thought about it till I had kids myself, then I thought, 'Poor Mam!' I still have some letters from Mam, seventy years old, that she wrote to me when I was in Carlisle hospital for two months. Reading them recently, it was like Mam was here again.

Jenny Doran and her twin sister Lily, who died in infancy.

When I met my husband Billy, I'd had an accident with my eye. I was seventeen and I worked at Edgard's. They made uniforms for the forces and I was taking some stitches out when the scissors flew up into my eye. It was bandaged for months. Billy had been out with my brother-in-law for a drink and he fetched Billy over to Mam's to meet her. I was there and that's how Billy met me. He always said he fell in love with a lass who had a patch on her eye!

Edgard's was at Catherine Mill first, then later at Preston Street. We had great fun in that grim old mill. The lasses put notes in the coat pockets for the servicemen to find; my sister that was killed, she worked in the leather room and got writing to this lad in the Air Force. Then she got married and wrote and told him she was passing him on to her younger sister. He first wrote to me, 'Dear Jenny', then it got to be, 'My Dear Jenny,' and then, 'Dearest Jenny!' But I started going out with Billy and he said, 'You can pack that up!'

Billy was a great lad, one of the best. I married him when I was nineteen and we lived with my mam at Woodhouse. But Billy hated it, he didn't like living in. He was always wandering the streets in the evening looking for lodgings for us. Anyway, we got this old house at Sunny Hill, it really was old, you know, and we were in that two and a half year. We were only with my mam six months before we got that. Ladypit cottages. There's a long line of garages on it now, below Harras Moor hill.

It was a poor area. The best of it, this old lady who owned the cottages, Billy went to see her and she let him have one, but unbeknownst to us, they were already condemned. One up, one down, stairs curved up out of the downstairs room. No door on the bedroom - you just stepped off the stairs straight in t' the room. No back door, just one at the front. It was ancient. We cooked, ate, lived, in the one room downstairs. There was a toilet a few yards down the lane for all the cottages to use, all eight of them, and a washhouse. The lighting was an oil lamp. The minute you lit it, well – I'll tell you this: I used to walk from there down to Whitehaven with the pram and then up to Woodhouse to see my mam and then back again. I thought nothing of it. I would come in and light the lamp and then all the cockroaches would run, scuttling away in all directions. DDT had just come out and every Friday I would put it all round the skirting board. The neighbours started complaining that, for some reason, they were getting twice as many cockroaches as usual! One of the cottages was deserted and there was a nest of rats living in an old armchair in there.

Valley School Dinner Ladies. Jenny Doran far left, with colleagues Pauline Hartley and Joan. In front is Brenda. Joan and Brenda's surnames are unknown.

I often wondered how I stuck it, but we were as happy as larks, so happy, because there was just us two. We paid four shillings and tuppence a week rent, but when the rent man first came he wouldn't take owt and for four months that went on and then he decided to accept the rent. We were relieved because we felt secure then. He said we were squatters, so him taking the rent made it more official, we thought.

Our first council house was on the 09 side of Mirehouse, on

Skiddaw Road. Over the road from us was just fields; part of the top of Meadow Road hadn't been built on yet. Part of Bowfell Road was there, and Melbreak Close. That was in1950. Me and Billy were married in '47 and got a house three years later. There was no bridge across the railway then, so the two halves of the Mirehouse estate hadn't been joined together, you couldn't get across to the other side. I think they must have been working on the bridge at that time. I already had Brenda and was pregnant with June when we moved in. When I went into labour, my Billy had to run all the way up the hill to St Bees Road, then across to Greenbank, because there was no telephone box down here then, that was the nearest.

Mirehouse Pond was a proper lake before they divided it, full of weeds. It's not as nice now as it was then. You used to see foxes if you went walking round there and there was a lot of wildlife. When we lived over that side of Mirehouse the workmen had a great big long hut and they used to let us have social evenings in it. We'd have tea dances; George Clements used to come over with a gramophone to play records for us.

Billy was a miner. He loved first shift but he had to get up at quarter past four to walk to work up at Haig. There were no buses to get there. Seven years we lived in Skiddaw Road and were happy, but Billy had always fancied a pub and he put in for one: The Crown Inn at Hensingham. It's a boxing club now. Mam went mad: 'You've nivver even been in a pub!' she said to me. But I didn't want Billy to say later that I stopped him having the chance. Eighteen months we were there. He loved it, but he'd still t' work at the pit because it didn't pay. I worked in the pub in the day, Billy came in at two o'clock from the pit and he went straight in to the bar, and I went to make his dinner. I hated it there, so we gave up in the end.

We were fortunate, when we came out of the pub, to get this house on Link Road. There was a bus driver, Jimmy McMean, he was a conservative councillor and he got us this house. He was my hero for helping us then. That was 1957 and I've been in here since. There were about twenty trees on that green outside once; it was like a little wood. Now they've chopped them down; there's only three left.

I went to be a dinner lady when we moved back to Mirehouse, first at Hensingham School, then Valley. I was a dinner lady thirty years and I loved it; I still meet young people in their forties now and they say, 'You were my dinner lady!' When I retired I came home laden with presents and Billy said, 'I'm so proud of you!'

Sundays, we went to St Andrew's Church. Services were in the school till the church was built. Billy was a 'sides' person in the church, I was a volunteer cleaner. The vicar, Reverend Forward, helped me do the dusting one Wednesday because nobody else had come. He just joined in - I was so embarrassed. The Calder Club was on our door step, Billy's favourite place for a night out. It was brilliant on a Saturday night. I remember walking home in stocking feet from there because my stilettos were killing me. I've always written poetry and wrote one about the Calder Club. Often in the evening Billy would be reading the paper and I'd say, 'Billy, I wrote another poem,' and he'd sigh and put the paper down and look fed up. I'd read it to him and ask, 'What do you think then?' and he would say, 'Aye, it's awright.'

Billy was a councillor for a lot of years. He just wanted to help people and got no pay for it, except for the last two years. A man called Proud at the pit was always on at Billy to put in for the council and so he did and was on the council for eleven years from 1966. Some of the houses had gone downhill a bit by then. One day, two ladies came to talk to Billy; I always stayed out of the way in the kitchen when people came to see him. When they went Billy was on the phone about it; they'd complained about creepy things coming out of the wallpaper. He phoned Mr Blanchard, the housing manager, and he said, 'You know what they are, Billy? Bugs!' Some of the houses had got infested.

Jenny and her husband, Billy Doran.

Another time, a young married couple had been offered a house and, as the paper said, it was a house 'not fit for pigs!' Billy was just going to work when they rang. He was on back shift this day and had put his bait up and the phone rang as he was going out. This couple wanted him to go and look at the house they'd been allocated on Newlands Avenue. Well, after he saw it, he never got to work: he went to the Council and the *Whitehaven News*, because the house was so terrible. The rooms were filled with rubbish bags full of stripped wallpaper; there was broken glass, paint tins, all over the house. The coal house door was hanging off, no door handles, the ceiling was about to collapse. It was mouse infested and the workmen had left broken windows and rubbish in the garden. Council's own workmen left it like that! In the end, the couple got offered another house. But at the pit, if you didn't get in a full week, you lost your bonus. So Billy lost a day's pay for helping that family and his bonus as well. We were hard up that week! He went to the council to see if he could claim it back, but they told him he shouldn't have done it in his own work time!

When the kids were small we hired a bungalow at Caulderton in the summer, but later we went abroad. Billy loved holidays. He was never bothered about the house. He used to say, 'Any money we've got, we're having holidays while we're together.'

33 Lakeland Ave
Woodhouse
Whitehaven

Dear Jennie just a line hoping
you are feeling not so bad
Violet has just been on the
Phone to see how you are I hear
you have gone through your
operation and you were
fairly comfortable I have
just sent you a parcel off
with your flannel, & a small
towel, soap, Sanitary towels,
rations, a few sweets, Bar
of Chocolate, 2 pears, (apple
from Mrs Horrocks, and a
little rum butter and a little
cake) tomatoes, I think every
body has been to ask after
you, Nora, Ettie, Betty Wilkins
Sadie Thomson, Violet Casson,
Jean Thomson Mrs Leary,
Mrs Kearney. Daddie and

I will be up to see you on Saturday George and I did not get home until quarter to nine we had to wait until six Oclock from Carlisle. Well lass I hope you are feeling better and it wont be long until you are home, Violet and George Stayed all night so I will close now with love from all at home and kisses from your Mam + Dad nellie, Violet George

P.S hope you get parcel alright and dont answer in case you hurt your eye

Letter to Jenny Doran from her mother, written 25th September 1944 and sent to the Cumberland Infirmary in Carlisle. Jenny was in hospital recovering from an injury to her eye. Food rationing was in place so items for Jenny's parcel would not have been easy to come by.

I'm glad, because I have all those memories: Marjorca, Malta, Spain, Greece. In 1974 we went for over a month to Russia and the Black Sea, all paid for by the Russian miners. We had a doctor and interpreter that travelled with us and got given fifty roubles per family to spend. There was a chance for twenty families to go from Haig Pit, but only three put their names forward. I think people were scared because the Russians were communists. Joe and Joan Norman, Jack and Florence Holliday, and both couples' children came with us. The best bit was, when we got back, the pit had all Billy's wages waiting for him to pick up!

When we were on holiday in Marjorca, one time, the courier asked would we like another four days extra, for free. We knew there was a catch - they'd overbooked the planes! When we got back Billy went up t' Haig Pit to check what shift he was on and came back and said, 'The pit's closing, I've been offered redundancy.'

I said, 'What do you wanna do, lad?'

He said two words, 'I'm tired.'

So I said, 'Finish then, it's alright with me.'

Right, left and centre, they were going off sick, but Billy wouldn't. He said, 'I'll walk out o' that pit, the way I walked in.' So he stayed for the last three months and, do you know, he was carried out with a smashed hip! That's why he packed in the Council as well. Forty-four years in the pit, he was.

All Billy's family had worked in the mines. Billy's dad was the last one to be brought out of William Pit in 1947. One hundred and four men died in that disaster. He lost his favourite brother at Haig. Another brother lost an arm, a brother lost fingers and another died from injuries at eighteen. The pits took a lot off him. We were just married in the March 1947 and William Pit went up in the August. Billy and I were on the shore, down Barrowmouth, off from Woodhouse. We were walking and met someone who said there'd been a big explosion. Billy knew his dad was on that shift, so we hurried over to his mam. They wouldn't let Billy and his brother down on rescue; when they knew they had family down there, they chased them off. There were so many to be buried, they had to have mass funerals every day for a good while after.

Billy's dad was a proper character. Duffy Doran, he was known as. He did poaching and all kinds of things. He never got dressed up proper, except for our wedding, when he borrowed a suit, one of the lads' shirts, and the tie off another. He won the Military Medal in the First World War. Billy's mother always kept the medal in pride of place on the mantelpiece. During that week the pit went up, all sorts of people were coming and going to her house and the medal went missing. It's never been seen since. Billy and I went to Carlisle and went round all the pawn shops to try and find it for her, but we never got it back. Billy's dad wouldn't tell us what he'd won it for, but not long ago a fella got in touch with Billy's brother, saying he was trying to find out more about the man who saved his dad's life. And that was Billy's dad, Duffy Doran.

Jenny Doran

Everyone Fitted In

I was born in 1926 in Spennymoor, County Durham. Dad was Scottish but he went to work in Spennymoor as a fitter, where he married my mother. We'd a two up, two down house. There were eleven of us living there, nine kids and my parents. The man who lived two doors away asked us to rent his house, so we moved up two houses. It had been his mother's and she'd died. Our house had one of them old fashioned compost toilets with a wooden seat. Later on we got one that had a flush, but it was still outside!

I came to West Cumbria in 1949, when I was twenty-three. I'd married and Arthur belonged t' Maryport. I met him in the forces when I was in the equipment section at the RAF Poddington base, near Northampton. When we were both demobbed, we came to live with his sister in Workington. There was a cloth factory there where I worked mending the fabric.

Later on, we moved to Whitehaven, because Arthur got a job with the Gas Board and it was too far to travel from Maryport. Whitehaven was busier than Spennymoor, and more crowded. The houses seemed closer together. The harbour had engines running up and down all the time and coal was loaded up on to boats. The kids played on the little bit of beach called the Golden Sands; I don't know if it was ever golden, but that beach seemed to get dirtier *after* the mines closed. Men used to go picking coal off the beach; there were fishing boats and a shop selling fish; the Quaker Oats factory, and Smiths both used to be there. It was really lively. There were three cinemas in Whitehaven, as well, the Queen's, the Gaiety and the Empire. There was sometimes a panto on at the Queen's, before the Civic Hall was built.

We lived on Roper Street for a bit, renting two rooms in a man's house for our lodgings. We waited four and a half years to get a council house and in1953, just before the coronation, we moved in to Ashness Close. We had to wash the floor two or three times to get rid of the mud left from the workmen's boots! It was just bare walls, fresh plastered; we couldn't paint for a year, it was that new. The rent was nineteen shillings and tuppence, but it went up to nineteen and ten pence soon after.

Everybody was friendly and of a summer night the women all went up t' the old lady's house at the end of the row. We'd sit outside talking, five of us, and we took turns making cake and tea. People often sat out on their doorsteps then, on nice evenings. Mostly it was young married couples living here. Down in the bottom, on Mirehouse Road, they were still building. After the war, a lot of people lived in rooms, or with their parents, so the houses were needed.

My husband went to Sellafield in 1955 and stayed there for thirty-two years. Everyone wanted to work there! His pay went up three pounds a week, from eight

Laura Reed in 1946.

to eleven pounds! That made a big difference; he didn't want me to work and I couldn't, anyway, after Alison was born because she needed a lot of care. I had Janet first, then Alison. Alison was born disabled. Nurse Beatty, the district nurse came in two or three times a week to make sure I was managing ok, but that was all the help I got. Alison died when she was five. She was always very light, but I was so pleased when I managed to get her weight up to two stone! Then she started falling back. She went into hospital one day and died the next. Her lungs never developed properly, and one of them was always very small.

In the early days, there wasn't much to do on the estate, no bingo or anything. I made all the

Laura Reed (front) and RAF friends stationed in Kinloss, Scotland 1946.

children's clothes, even a coat once, and that kept me busy. You had to walk to the pond for the bus to town. Mostly things were on t' other side of the estate. Sometimes we went to Whist Drives in the Calder Club; Pam Robinson ran them on Wednesday nights. After Alison was born, I started going to St Andrew's Church and I took her with me in a special pram I'd got from the NHS. We walked a lot: we walked the estate in the evening and got to know other people. You'd stop and have a crack with them. Janet, my daughter used to walk to Valley School with her friend, Linda. I took her the first day and went to pick her up later and she said, "What you doing here, mam?"

I said, "I came for you!" But she knew her way home alright and wanted to do it by herself, and there was hardly any traffic then.

I was here on my own for years, with my family in County Durham, but after a bit two of my brothers came over. One was a fireman and rose up to be Assistant District Officer in the Fire Service, the other worked at Sellafield. There weren't many out of work then. People came from all over the country to work at Sellafield, but there was no bother; they just mixed in alright. Everyone fitted in.

Laura Reed

A Pocketful of Fish

Elizabeth Armstrong in 1941.

I don't belong Whitehaven originally; I'm from Preston. I was born Elizabeth Bell in 1924. There were six of us girls and a brother who died when he was fifteen months old. When we were having a friendly argument, Dad always said: 'I can't win with all you girls in the house!' Mum was from Frizington and moved to Preston to work in a pub. That's what a lot of women did in those days - went into service. She lived in on the job and that's how Dad met her; he used to go into the pub for a pint. She was called Elizabeth Anne Hayley.

Dad was Edward Bell; he came from a little village in Lancashire called Goosnargh. It's much bigger now. My grandparents lived next door to Goosnargh church. Granddad was a fine cabinet maker and made all the furniture for their house, and for the church. Dad's brother, Ernest, was in the army and the story goes that he was

Edward Bell, Elizabeth Armstrong's father, pictured here with his first wife and their daughters, Anne and Doris.

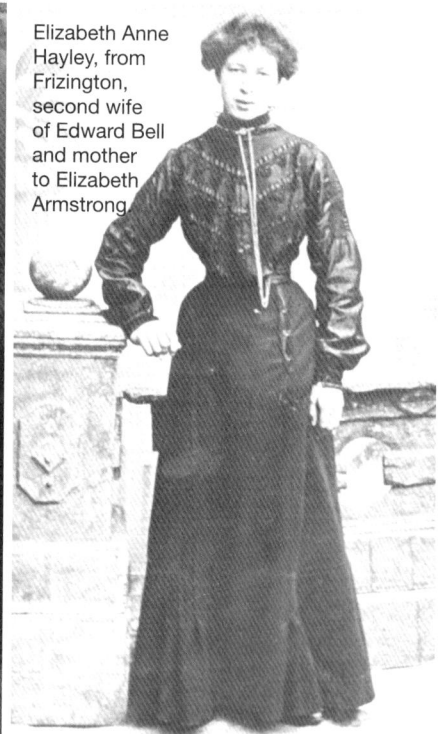

Elizabeth Anne Hayley, from Frizington, second wife of Edward Bell and mother to Elizabeth Armstrong.

Elizabeth Armstrong's wedding in Preston. Front row: John Armstrong left, Elizabeth, Ronnie Armstrong (John's brother), and chief bridesmaid, Agnes, Elizabeth's twin sister.

crossing a village on horseback one day, I don't know where he was, maybe Africa, and a crocodile got him. The officers all clubbed together and put up a plaque in Goosnargh church in remembrance of him. Dad was a plumber and worked at the Preston Gas Company. He worked Saturday morning and there was a big market there then, so he used to stop to buy all the fruit and sweets for the week on the way home, but we were only allowed two sweets a day!

Dad had been married before, but he lost his wife and one daughter, who died when she was only five. Then he married my mum and she died as well, and my brother. I was a twin and Mum died when me and my sister were only two days old. It was much riskier having children in those days. The doctor didn't even know Mum was having twins, because I was born first and then he said, 'Oh my goodness, there's another one!' After Mum died, there was no one to look after us, so me and my twin sister had to go into a home and we lived there for about three years. Later, when Dad married Mum's sister, we went back home to live.

My stepmum used to come back to Cleator Moor and fetched us with her to visit the family; that's how I met my husband, John, on one of those trips. No honeymoon for us! We got married in Preston on a Saturday and came back to Whitehaven on the Sunday and moved into No.1 Lowther Street with John's parents. We were there until 1951 and had two children aged three and eighteen months by the time we got a house on Grisedale Close.

Some people had already moved in to Grisedale when we came, but not a lot, and they were still building on Whinlatter Road. Watsons, Farrers, Agnews, Cassons - they were some of the families living there then. We lived on Grisedale nearly fifty years. I remember, it was pouring down that day we moved in. John's mother came with us and my daughter, Susan, was running round excited and she said, 'Mum, we've got *two* toilets! There's one for you and one for me Nanna!'

The kids all went to Valley School. The first day I took Susan to school, she came home for her dinner and she couldn't believe that she had to go back to school again after! Susan got to love school, but Martin had a problem with it at first, so I used to go in. The teacher said to him, 'if I see your mother in this classroom again, I'll get the police!'

After that, when we got to the gate, he'd say, 'It's alright Mum, I'll go in from here.' A teacher wouldn't get away with saying that now. I used to ask him, 'What have you done today?' and he would answer, 'Nothing!', but he did alright.

Thinking back, I must have met my husband, John, in 1946, because I knew him when William Pit went up in '47. I'd come up for a holiday, but I never saw him all that week 'cause he was on the rescue team and down the mine all the time. John got all three medals for rescue work: bronze, silver and gold. His brother came running that day and said 'William Pit's gone up!' John had thought that might happen, because he said lately it'd been like a furnace down there. He was lucky he wasn't on shift when it went; John's mother always said, 'If John fell in the river, he'd come up with a pocketful of fish!' But he lost his brother- in-law in the accident, John Mowat. That was such a shame; he'd been in the army and come through the war, only to end up getting killed in the pit. When they found him, he was just sitting there bolt upright and only had one tiny little mark on his cheek. My John was so busy that week he was exhausted and just wanted to sleep when he came up top. It must have been so hard fetching all them men out.

William never opened again as a working pit after the explosion, but John went down for a long while after because they had to get as much machinery up as they could - it was all on hire. The day I had our first baby, John was at work, it was a Saturday. He was working with a friend of his who was going to a wedding that day when they finished work. John had just finished talking to him and turned to walk away, when a second later a great slab of stone came down and killed his friend. It was such a near miss for John. He'd nightmares for a long time after, but he never told me about it at the time, 'cos I was in hospital with the baby. When he told me later I said, 'Don't go back down again!', but he still went down and he moved on to Haig Pit when they finally cleared William. He said, 'I'm going to Haig' and I said, 'Have you not had enough yet?' At Haig, he had an accident and had to work on the top. He started having blackouts and got emphysema and that's what finally killed him.

When we first got married John said, 'I am the worker in this house!' so I didn't work for a long time, but I did go back to work eventually, when the kids were older. I went to Cleator Fasteners for a bit, then I was at Smith's at Hensingham and used to walk up there every day with Mrs Storey. I cleaned The Globe pub in Hensingham and I cleaned at Whitehaven College. What a lot of brass to polish there, all the doors had brass knobs! Before I got married I had all sorts of jobs - and to think today people can't get work! There was loads of work when I finished school. You finished school on the Friday and were working on the Monday. I ended up working building planes in the war at Dick Kerr's in Preston, near the docks. I'd to train newcomers what to do. I worked inside the planes doing all the wiring. Women had to do jobs like that in the war. After the war, I went to work for a factory that made airline runways. I was in the civil defence for a lot of years; the idea was to keep the country ready for if there was another war. In 1958 I got a civil defence tournament medal for a competition we won. The challenge was to see who could set up a field kitchen the fastest. We went all over the country doing competitions like that.

Elizabeth Armstrong

A Hand on my Shoulder

I lived on Croasdale Road in Mirehouse for fifty years. That's on the 09 side of Mirehouse, not the 06. We moved into the house in 1952. Before that, me and Chuck shared a house on the corner of George Street and Queen Street for two-and-a-half years. We shared with another family: they had the front room, the parlour, and one of the upstairs bedrooms and we had the back room and a bedroom. The old house had a tiny kitchen, sometimes with cockroaches and mice running about, but the worst thing was the cobbled yard. The stones were so big and slippery you could hardly walk on them. We paid about six shillings a week for that.

At that time, I worked at Edgard's. Thirty-two years I worked there altogether. Mam and my sister used to come down from the Valley and my sister would look after Sandra. There were quite a few women in the same circumstance as me, married but working part-time. I was a machinist and a hand sewer for a long time, but they moved you about to different jobs. Mrs Ross - her and her husband came from London to manage the factory. There were about four or five hundred women and a few lads. Mrs Ross, she never had family of her own and she said she was mother to everybody in the factory. She liked to be involved in your life. There were the three brothers who owned it: Leo was in charge of the office, Derek taught us how to machine, and Dave was involved with getting the orders for uniforms. Mrs and Mr Ross had a flat in Cross Street. Mrs Ross sent for us and said Harry had took up photography and wanted to take some portraits, so she picked about half dozen of us and he took photos and Mam was chuffed to bits to get one. They always said whoever took over pushed Mrs Ross out. I don't know about that, but I know the factory was her life and she was very fair.

I was adopted when I was born. My real mother already had a little boy, Desmond. He was two years old when I was born. Then Dad died. This happened in Preston, mind, but I didn't know that till later on – that's another story, I'll come back to that. Mother, she got involved with this guy who had a coal business and they called him Miller. He was partners in Miller & Batty, well known coal merchants. She got married and I got adopted, I don't know why. I didn't get to know anything about that family. She kept Desmond.

I don't know how my mother ended back in Whitehaven. She lived on George Street for a bit and that's where I lived when I was a kid. My adopted parents, Annie and Henry Rothery, lived down a cul de sac off George Street called Banks Lane. Further up were the bigger, more expensive houses. One day, I was twanging the rope, skipping with my friends. We'd to put the rope down to let my real mother pass over and one of Mam's friends said, 'Put it round her bloody neck!' Well, I couldn't wait t' run home and tell Mam because you weren't allowed to swear!

Later, my real mother had a house on Duke Street, next to the pub on the corner, and opposite Brookes's. Mr Miller had died - I don't think they were married many years. When I was fourteen, or fifteen, me and the lasses would go about town all dressed up on a Saturday and she'd always be standing on the step with Desmond when I walked past. The lasses would say, 'Sadie she's watching yer'. If I caught her eye, I would just turn my head away. I always knew she was my mother, Mam told me as soon as I was old enough to understand. Kids used to say to me, 'Yer mother never wanted yer!'

Well it took your confidence away knowing that. I would cry, but Mam would say, 'You *are* wanted, Sadie, we *chose* you. We picked you, because we wanted you.'

I had a happy childhood and my family were happy with me. My sister was a bit jealous; she'd say 'Dad always gives you the top of his egg!' Now *that* was an honour. Dad was a miner. He was ill a long time, but I don't know what was wrong with him. Mam had to look after the family when he died. He died when I was six and I'd a sister that died a month before my dad. Mam had five of her own family when she adopted me. Our family hadn't much money; we just got by week to week.

Harry was the eldest in our family. He was a perfect lad, too perfect. He got killed. He used to come home on leave, he was one of the cooks in the army, and he brought all sorts home for Mam. I relished those days he came home - his sweet ration was for me! He died in April. I was sixteen, so I don't know, maybe it was 1943. How it happened was, he was on embarkation leave, they gave you that before you were going abroad, and when he went back to camp they sent him down south, instead. That happened again and one of Mam's so called friends said, 'Is he still here? Has he seen no fighting yet?' It got to him, because he was a sensitive sort of guy, so when he went back he volunteered to go to Burma. Out there, they went into this village the Japanese had just evacuated and Harry was pulling the Japanese flag down to put the British one up when a sniper shot him. I remember

Sadie Nicholson, photo taken to put in her brother Demond's wallet when he was in the forces.

them coming to our house with a flag for Mam to put in the electricity shop window on Lowther Street in memory of him. My birthday is in April, as well. Two weeks after he died a parcel came for me with a beautiful pair of Japanese pyjamas inside for my birthday present. I could hardly bring myself to wear them! Harry was twenty-four when he died.

When my brother Desmond Wilkinson got to be about seventeen, he said to my adopted sister, 'Is Sadie my sister?'

She said, 'I think you should ask your mother about that!'

But he said, 'She won't talk about her.'

He was going into the Air Force and he came to my sister again and he said, 'Could you get a photo of Sadie to put in my wallet.' Mother couldn't really afford it, but she went down to Romney Studio in King Street and got two photos and let him have one. They started putting films on of a Sunday night in town and me and about four friends would go. The lads on leave from the forces would come to meet us there and, if Desmond was among them, he'd come up to me and quietly put a hand on my shoulder.

I'd such a powerful feeling towards him, I felt such a bond. It's maybe something in the blood, I can't explain it, but I think he felt the same towards me. Sometimes, I might be doing my shopping and Desmond would appear and say, 'if you just hold on there, I'll get the car,' and then he would bring me home. Things like that happened; he always seemed to appear. Odd times at Braystones beach, Desmond would turn up and say, 'I'll run you and the kids home, Sadie.' And he told his family about me. They used to speak to me, which was nice, and when his eldest daughter got married his wife said to me, 'I'm very sorry, Sadie, we'd love to invite you,' but my mother was still alive then and they didn't want to cause any trouble.

Mother ended up living in a big house in Maryport and that's where she died. I was reading the *Whitehaven News* one day and all of a sudden these words seemed to come up from it and float out at me. It was the announcement of my mother's death. I felt so strange, because she'd died. One of her friends said that mother told her it was one of the biggest mistakes of her life, giving me up. That meant a lot to me, because it's a strange thing when you feel you're not wanted.

I'll tell you this, I've two daughters went to Canada to live and we decided to go there on holiday. So we went down to see about birth certificates to get passports. Well, Chuck already had his and we got the ones for the kids ok, but when it came to mine the woman said, 'We don't have one for you.'

I said, 'Does that mean I'm not here?'

The kids said, 'Don't worry, Mam, we'll tell you all about it when we come back!' Dry humour, like their dad. Later, I got a letter from the registrar to say she'd finally found me: born in Preston! Now that was a bit of a shock, to find that out. I don't know how that came about.

Talking about passports reminds me, after we got them we went to France a few times. Chuck was a Normandy veteran and he liked to go and visit the war cemeteries. The last time we went James Tweedy was with us. He'd looked for a long time trying to find the grave of his best friend, but had never had any luck. He was just saying to me, 'I don't think I'm ever going to find him, Sadie,' when there it was! The grave was right in front of us! James's eyes filled up with tears, 'At last!' he said, 'I've found him at last!' It meant such a lot to him.

When my family lived off George Street, Mam used to clean The Anchor pub. Later, I took that job over on a Sunday morning to get money to give her. The pub's gone now; it belonged to Duke Waddington. The couple that lived next door, every

Sadie and Chuck Nicholson during their courting days in 1948.

Chuck Nicholson, war veteran, in his army uniform.

Friday night they would have a row, 'cos he'd had a couple of drinks and he'd throw her and her suitcase out in t' the yard. They lived together and that was a big thing then. She'd go back in, though, before the night was out. Bonfire night he'd run out with a frying pan with an egg in it and cook it on the bonfire.

Sometimes he would look through his window, see someone and say, 'I hate that fella!', and put his fist through the window! Other times, he'd light a paper and put it under the pub door to try and set fire to it, but it would just go out.

How I met Chuck was when I went to a friend's birthday party one Easter. Chuck was very, very shy, so he asked his friend to ask me to go for a walk with him on Good Friday. I said 'Yes,' but his friend walked in the middle of us all the time we were out! Chuck told me that when he was sixteen and working in Smith's, where they stored all the paper, he used to watch me going by on my way to Edgard's and say, 'That's who I'm going to marry.'

I always liked to dance. I have a lot of trophies and, unknown to me, Chuck had secret dance lessons so he could dance with me. We went to the Empire Ballroom every Saturday. In the war, they used to have dancing in Lowther Park as well; they put boards over the grass for a dancefloor, it was fantastic. There were bands playing in the bandstand. Lots of people gathered in the park and lads on leave would come down and join in the dancing. Mother used to say, 'Why don't yer tek your bed down there!', because I was there every day. During the war we used to put on parties sometimes. Mrs McCluskey, Josie Todd's mother, and a few of us would get together and put a party on in a room on Charles Street; we sometimes showed bits of movies.

Anyway, me and Chuck were courting about four and a half years and got married in 1950. Chuck was in the building trade. He worked for McGuffy's and then the council doing house repairs and maintenance. He loved working on the sites. A lot of the lads he worked with would take him on their 'foreigners' - extra jobs in the building trade done at weekends, or evenings. He saved up the money for our holidays from those jobs.

When I had our Sandra, I was in the old hospital. She had a mop of thick black hair and was about six pounds summat. There was this big lass, a nurse; she'd come off a farm and walked like a farmer. She'd go up and down the ward saying, 'I hate this job!' Well, those days they kept all the babies together in a nursery and then they'd bring them out to you to feed them. She gave me this baby and it was a boy, bald as a coot and about nine pounds odd. I said, 'This is not my baby!', and she said, 'It was the only one left!'

The woman who was holding Sandra said, 'Oh, I thought mine had grown hair ovvernight.'

So I said, 'What, and lost three pounds and had a sex change as well!' I've often thought since, I'm sure there were a lot of women then who must've gone home with the wrong baby.

I made three rag rugs for moving into Croasdale Road. We had nice neighbours and we always had a good laugh. There are only two of the originals left now. My old neighbour, Malcolm, lived next door for fifty odd years and he still picks me up and takes me to church every Sunday and brings me home again. Our house was built with bricks from the brickworks on Low Road. One side of the road was all built with bricks, the other side with blocks. When we moved to Mirehouse there was just two shops: Josie Todd's was the grocer's and the other was a fish shop. Different days the mobile shops came: Masons with milk, Maypole's on Friday with butter and cheese. You had a pantry with a big stone slab that kept things cool, but they went when the houses were renovated. Nothing went bad, but we bought regular, not stocking up for the week like now. There were no buses, the roads were rough, not levelled or tarmacked. It's helped us in later life, all this walking; I still walk down to town every day. I'm used to it.

Behind the houses there was waste ground called the Back Field and on Friday afternoon a few of us used to go and play bingo out there for a couple of shillings, having a laugh in the fresh air. The insurance man used to come to our house and knock and, if there was no answer, he'd walk straight in and through the house, the doors were always open, and come over to the field for his money. My husband

Whitehaven Coronation Party Committee1953. Centre front, Josie Todd. To her right, Maggie Sanderson (daughter of Duke Waddington). Centre of second row, Mrs Canavan and Mr McCormack. Next to him, Sadie Nicholson. Photo courtesy of Sadie Nicholson.

Line Dancing in Whitehaven Castle Park. Front right, Teresa Guise and behind her Sadie Nicholson. Photo courtesy of Sadie Nicholson and taken approx.1990.

used to say, 'He shouldn't have come in without someone openin' the door.'

My mother lived with us for eight years; Chuck was happy for her to be with us. One room had four bunk beds for the girls; Stephen had a room to his self, mother in the other room. Chuck bought a bed settee and we slept in the living room. The lasses used to say sitting on it was like sitting on the back of the bus! It wasn't comfortable, but it did the job. There was an insurance man came to the house who always had a cough. Mother would say, 'Get him a wee drop of whiskey to help his cough, Sadie.' Well, he had that cough for months; the whiskey bottle was going down and down and nobody else drank it! She always fell for it: 'Oh, he's still got that cough,' she'd say, and he used to go off with a smile on his face.

Some days the ragman used to come round Mirehouse with a horse and cart giving toys and balloons to the kids in exchange for rags. Our Anne used to play with a wee lad called Gerry. He'd pull her along on his trolley. She says one day, 'Mam, Gerry and me's got 'gaged.' She had a ring on her finger off the ragman. 'But Gerry's mam's gonna smack him,' says Anne, ''cos he took his dad's best jumper t' the ragman t' get the ring.'

Saturday mornings I'd get up at six and make pasties for a picnic. There would be about twelve adults and twenty-two kids from the road and we'd all go on the train from Corkickle to Braystones beach for the day. All the husbands would be waving from the bottom of the gardens saying, 'Thank God for that!' There was this old guy with a cap on at the station taking money and trying to count the kids and he'd say, 'I'm sure I counted more than that,' 'cos we'd only pay for maybe twelve of them. We'd come back around four o' clock. One particular time, we're stood on the station and the train whizzed on past us, so we all walked in procession to Nethertown. There was a bus on there because at that time there used to be the Tow Bar night club where the young 'uns went, so we managed to get a lift on that. The children loved those days. We took tea bags and got hot water from a wee shop on the beach, and there was fresh, cool spring water flowing down to the shore for the all the kids to drink.

Sadie Nicholson

Two Kinds of Horses

I've lived on Newlands Avenue over sixty-one years. When I got married, I used to go every week to the man at the council to try and get a house. People used to say once he got sick of you, you got a house! Mrs Dodsworth lived next door, she was a real lady. Her husband bought all the kids a jubilee mug, such kind people. Mrs Dodsworth and half the street came over to look at this house with me when I came to view it.

My husband worked for Laing's and their site office was right opposite where I live. He was a scaffolder and helped build these houses. We couldn't afford for him to carry on with that job when we had a family because he got laid off too much in bad weather and then there would be no money coming in, so he went to Sellafield.

Before we moved to Newlands in 1954, we lived with my mam on Greystone Road. Mam got the house when me and Edward were in Morecambe on honeymoon. My sister and her husband lived there as well and we both had a child each before we got our own houses, so Greystone Road was crowded. Mam and Dad slept in the little bedroom in a single bed

I grew up on George Street. Mam had a house on Woodhouse for a while, but we all got travel sick every time we went on the bus, so we had to give it up and move back into town, to 36 George Street, Mrs Murray's house. There were lots of little shops on George Street at one time: Eddie King's grocery store was there and Jackson's grocery. There was McGill's builders, a blacksmith who shoed horses through an archway, an old coaching spot, and two cloggers - Wigham's and Carty's. Katie Craddock, she was such a bonny little woman and lived with a fella called Jim; she'd a little shop sold yeast and sweets, maybe bread. She had a picture on her wall of herself when she was young and she was so beautiful, I always thought. The house where the McCormacks lived must have been a shop one time, because it had a window with Fry's Chocolate wrote in white on it. Arrighi's fish and chips were on the other side from us. You could buy lovely cakes at Mary Hetherington's on Scotch Street, Richardson's pies on Duke Street – the town was full of thriving shops.

Up on Peter's Street, there was a tanning yard. When the wagon came with the skins, it stunk. It was near St Jame's Church and the swinging field; I don't think they put any consideration into the fact that people were living so close by. We moved into a little house two doors off the swing field, but we couldn't sleep at night for the noise the rats were making running around. They were attracted there, maybe, because of the tannery.

My maiden name was Waddington and a relation of mine, Marmaduke Waddington, was in charge of the Town Hall. Another relative, my uncle Marmaduke, had The

Anchor pub on George Street and his son had The Beehive pub. Grandma had a pub, as well, called The Robin Hood. All the eldest lads in the Waddington family were called Marmaduke! Dad was the youngest in the family so he avoided the name!

Dad worked at William Pit, and at Haig and Lowca pits. He went to Marchon for a bit, but felt sick all the time he was there. William Pit was near us and all the miners would be coming and going past our house on their way to work. I was on my way to school when the 1941 explosion happened. Dad went down to help and come up with the body of John McGrievy. John Burney, my husband Edward's brother, was killed then. He was three weeks off being twenty-one. Twelve of them died.

Edward worked at William Pit when he was only fourteen. His Mam, Alice Burney, was invited to the Town Hall to meet the Duke of Kent after the 1941 explosion; it was a meeting for widows and mothers. The Duke of Kent asked if there was anything he could do for them and Alice spoke up, 'Yes, you can do something for me.' The war was on and, if you were in the pit, you couldn't leave. She asked the Duke to get Edward out of the pit because she'd already lost a husband and a son, and he did it for her. Edward

Alice Burney, Edward's mother, who lobbied for him to be released from the mining industry.

John Burney junior, brother to Betty Burney's husband, Edward. John was killed in the 1941 William Pit explosion.

John Burney senior, Military Medal winner, killed in Haig Pit in 1940.

came out of the pit and worked for the council for a bit, then went to work for a firm that made asbestos lagging for pipes. He spent some time in the army, as well, and went to the Far East. In later years, he got lung disease and Dr Telford wanted him to claim against the asbestos firm, but we didn't bother. The doctor came to check on him and he was in hospital regular, but the disease spread like lightning; the last four months he couldn't hardly breathe. We were fifty-nine years together.

John Burney the elder, Edward's dad, he won the Military Medal in the war. He'd held the line in France when the rest of the men were wounded, or killed. In 1919 he went to a ceremony in Carlisle for the medal and was presented with a gold watch and fifty pounds! A man called Mr Corkish got a medal at the same time, but not for the same thing. John had t' pawn the medal when times were hard during the 1926 miners' strike. When he went to Collis's to get it back, he was told there'd been a fire and it was destroyed! Edward went round museums for years after, in the hopes of finding it, but he thought it must have ended up in some private collection. John was killed at Haig Pit in1940: a pulley broke, wrapped round him and pulled his leg off and he died in hospital a few days later.

Me and the kids had a lucky escape once. When my sister, Lily, was big with her youngest, seven month gone, we went to William Pit beach with all the kids. There was my two and Lily's five. We went to Whitey Rock, between William Pit and Parton. We always sat on the right side of it for shade and shelter. The kids were enjoying

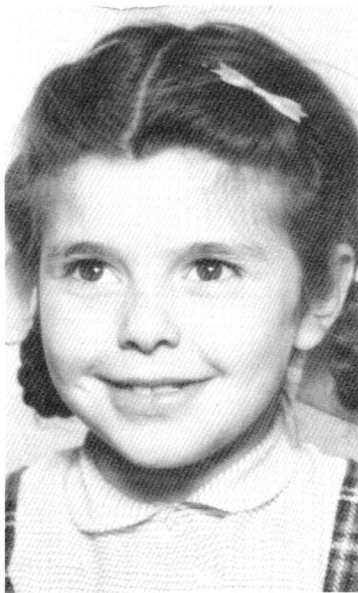

Maureen Burney, 4/11/1951 - 5/3/2015, daughter to Betty Burney, here aged eight.

swimming and we'd been there a fair while when these men started shouting at us from the path over by the railway, near Sempy's house on the Wagon Road. They were shouting: 'The tides comin' in; it's in on t'other side of the rock!' Well, there was no way off the beach except under the railway line! We'd to crawl through some sort of sewage, or drainage pipe. I went first, on account of Lily was pregnant and there might be rats. Lily came up last, with the kids in the middle. I got through part way, but the pipe branched off in different directions. I was in a panic; I didn't have a clue which way to go, so just kept going straight on! Thankfully, it was the right way, the pipe was dry and we met no rats! The fellas helped us out at t' other end, but we were so relieved we forgot to even ask their names!

I met Edward in the Empress Ballroom; he couldn't dance, but never mind. But they spoiled the Empress and made it into a sale room. My aunty put all her lovely rugs from The Anchor pub

NUMBER

HBGC   125 · 3   SURNAME
CHRISTIAN NAMES (First only in full)   BURNEY

ELIZABETH.

CLASS CODE
A

FULL POSTAL ADDRESS

11 GREYSTOKE CLOSE HBG.
MIREHOUSE.   WHITEHAVEN
HOLDER'S SIGNATURE
E Burney

CHANGES OF ADDRESS. No entry except by National
Registration Officer, to whom removal must be notified.

REMOVED TO (Full Postal Address)

FOR OFFICIAL ENTRY ONLY (apart from Holder's Signature).
MARKING OR ERASURE, IS PUNISHABLE BY

REMOVED TO (Full Postal Address)

NOTICE   HH 689354

1. **Always carry your**
Identity Card. You may be
required to produce it on
demand by a Police Officer in uniform or member of
H.M. Armed Forces in uniform on duty.

2. **You are responsible for this Card, and must**
not part with it to any other person. You must
report at once to the local National Registration Office if
it is lost, destroyed, damaged or defaced.

3. If you find a lost Identity Card or have in your
possession a Card not belonging to yourself or anyone in
your charge you must hand it in at once at a Police
Station or National Registration Office.

4. Any breach of these requirements is an offence
punishable by a fine or imprisonment or both.

FOR AUTHORISED ENDORSEMENTS ONLY

51-266

NATIONAL
REGISTRATION

IDENTITY
CARD

Betty Burney's ID
card.

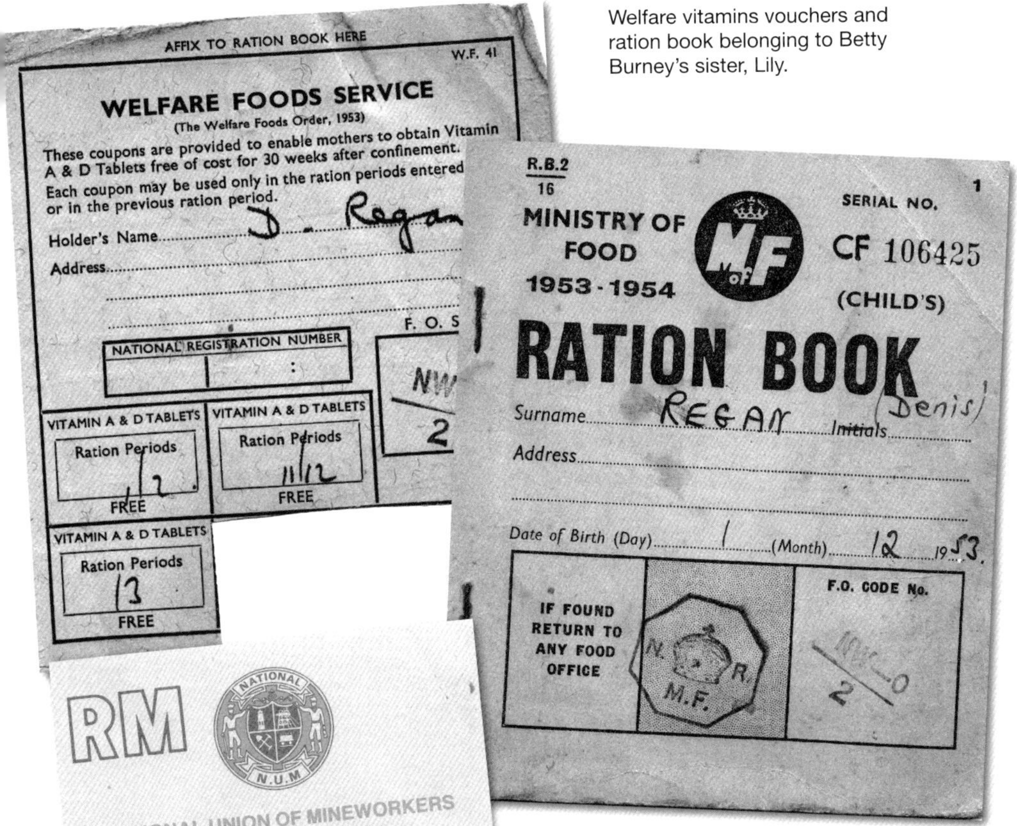

Welfare vitamins vouchers and ration book belonging to Betty Burney's sister, Lily.

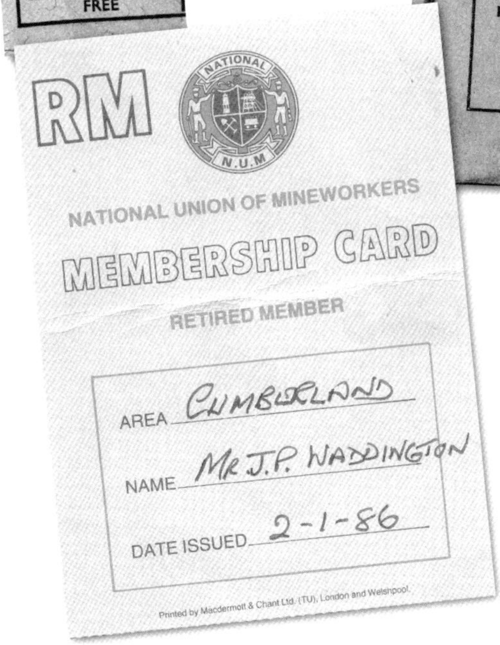

AFFIX TO RATION BOOK HERE
W.F. 41

WELFARE FOODS SERVICE
(The Welfare Foods Order, 1953)

These coupons are provided to enable mothers to obtain Vitamin A & D Tablets free of cost for 30 weeks after confinement. Each coupon may be used only in the ration periods entered or in the previous ration period.

Holder's Name........J_ Regan

Address.................................

NATIONAL REGISTRATION NUMBER
:

F.O.S

NW
2

VITAMIN A & D TABLETS	VITAMIN A & D TABLETS
Ration Periods	Ration Periods
7	11 12
FREE	FREE

VITAMIN A & D TABLETS
Ration Periods
1
FREE

R.B.2
16

1

MINISTRY OF FOOD
1953-1954

SERIAL NO.
CF 106425

(CHILD'S)

RATION BOOK

Surname....REGAN....Initials.... (Denis)

Address.................................

Date of Birth (Day).....1....(Month)...12...19 53.

IF FOUND RETURN TO ANY FOOD OFFICE

N.R. M.F.

F.O. CODE No.
NW-0 2

RM NATIONAL N.U.M.

NATIONAL UNION OF MINEWORKERS

MEMBERSHIP CARD

RETIRED MEMBER

AREA....CUMBERLAND

NAME....MR J.P. WADDINGTON

DATE ISSUED....2-1-86

Printed by Macdermott & Chant Ltd. (TU), London and Welshpool.

The NUM membership card of Betty Burney's father, Joseph Waddington.

into the sales. The Edgards, who came to Whitehaven to set up their factory, they bought up rugs and nice furniture for their flats from there. You could get some good furniture in the sale, but mostly what people had was the cheap utility furniture, poor quality wood.

I worked a lot of years at Edgard's and that got me interested in learning dressmaking, so me and eight of the women from work went one time and did dressmaking classes at the college. I made a lot of the children's clothes after that. Me and Mrs Ross, at Edgard's, we used to have little tiffs, but they were soon forgot. She sent for me to come back to work for her when Maureen was eighteen months old. When she was in bed badly once, she sent a message to see if I would go to the flat and visit her. She gave me a little box, all plush, with egg spoons in it when I married Edward. I left the factory and went to clean at the hospital for a while, but soon came back. She said to me, 'Betty there's two kinds of horses: one to do rough, heavy work, and the gentle kind. You are the gentle kind.' They came from Distington, Workington, all over to work there.

Betty Burney

Betty Burney, left, on holiday in Blackpool approx.1947. Centre is her close friend, Ada Scowcroft, and Mary Rogan is on the right. Ada died aged just twenty-one from TB, along with a number of other work colleagues from Edgard's, including Ethel Burney, Mary Holliday and Florrie Valery. There must have been some concern for the wellbeing of employees at the factory, as Betty recalls a van coming to the workplace to X-ray workers for signs of the disease.

Flowing Like a Waterfall

I am seventy years old and I've lived on Copeland Avenue over twenty-eight years now. My husband John died seven years back, at sixty-three, but the last twenty years he wasn't very good. The breathing trouble started after his triple bypass. He was a hod carrier all his life and he was always a healthy colour, so we couldn't understand why he got breathing problems. People were shocked; all his working life he was always running up and down a ladder. John and I had five daughters, three in two years. Now I've five grandsons, five granddaughters, three great granddaughters and one great grandson - so I've done my bit to keep things going! There's never a dull moment: the great grandkids, they always come around. We spent a lot of time helping rear grandkids; we had them every weekend. One just lives round the corner from me now. I hope I'll still be alive to be a great, great grandmother!

The house I live in now, I used to play in it when Mirehouse was being built. Before these houses, there were just fields and cows. There was a trough at the bottom of our garden where the cows would gather. There was a farmhouse nearby and a wee path going down past it, Leece's farm. It was all still countryside.

Before I lived on Copeland Avenue John and me lived on Greenbank estate. We'd lots of family around us. John was a Greenbank lad: his mam, his nan, his aunt, all of them lived there. I was eight when my family moved to Greenbank and my mam and dad lived there till they passed away.

My maiden name was Moore and my parents lived in old Newtown, where the Whitehaven Sorting Office is now. Our front door was where the machines are for sorting your letters. They were terraced houses. We had a sitting room that was dark, dark, dark. There wasn't a lot of room between the rows, so our house was overshadowed by the row of houses in front of us. The houses were small: you walked through the front door right into your sitting room. There wasn't any passageway, so you walked straight from there into the kitchen, which was dismal because there were no windows in it. To the right there was a winding staircase that came out of the kitchen and outside a toilet in the yard. The kitchen had a big black fireplace with a built-in oven. That sticks in my head. We had no carpets down, just bare boards in the bedrooms, I remember. Those houses were infested with cockroaches, and other things! I remember having to go to the soup kitchens on Irish Street with a tin with a lid on and I'd fetch the soup over home. I was five or six, so it was about 1950. It was just after the war, there were still rations. I remember the ration books and the gas masks - you had them in the house ready. If a bomb had dropped anywhere near us we would have gone up, because the house was all gas! Gas mantle lights. In the back, where there was no window, even in the gaslight it was dark.

When we went to Greenbank we thought we were posh because we had a bathroom and it was a parlour house. I have four sisters and two brothers, so there were seven of us. My younger brother was two when we moved and he cried, wanting to go home. Three bedrooms! Mam and Dad slept in the parlour. Best move ever for my mam. Dad wasn't keen but he was in the army, so not there constant.

Upstairs in the new house we could spread out, so we didn't need to have four of us in a bed. The girls, we had two rooms between us till my grandma came to live with us, then we had to go back in one room. We'd a double bed and a single bed, so whoever got the single bed first was happy! We didn't have a lot of furniture. We'd a big old fashioned wardrobe, but there wasn't much in it because we didn't have owt. I can remember we had a kind of straw mat on the first bit of the stairs till it curved round, then the rest was bare, and the bedrooms were bare. Mam didn't take much furniture from the house because of all the bugs and that. She got some utility furniture, but I don't know where she got it. It was the coalman who moved us, he took our stuff and we walked up to the hill to the new house, past the Workhouse that was still there. We knew a few people in there. One man, Maurice, took somebody in from the Workhouse. He got a house next to John Lasant and gave a man called Hugo a home.

Up at Woodhouse there wasn't a proper road, just a cinder track up to the estate. On Mirehouse hill the road there was tarmac. When I was young we played in the road; the game was 'bust the tar bubble'. We went home a right mess and got many a hiding, I can tell you! We used to play in the woods as well, where we had swings. Children today are in the house sitting at the television or computer, but we weren't allowed to stay in; you got up, had your breakfast and you were out. You knew your mealtimes and that was it!

When I first left school I went to Edgard's to work and I worked there, on and off, for many years. I was on specials seaming the big black overcoats; they were real heavy and it was hard work. At that time, there were jobs all round. There was Sekers, Kangol Ware, you had your pick. Now you can't get jobs. You could leave a job one day and start another the next.

For twenty-eight and a half years I worked at Smurfit's, up near the fire station. We made boxes: fancy boxes at Christmas for Harrods, washing powder boxes, whiskey boxes. After twenty-five years' service they gave me a watch and a bouquet of flowers. Then in the evening a taxi picked us up and took us to the restaurant where Zest is and the boss was there! We had a great night with a taxi laid on to take us back home. Smurfit's was called Matin and Lawson then. It was part of Smith's and it was real good money. Sellafield, Smiths, Marchon, they were the ones where you wanted to work, but I wasn't expecting to stop that long! When I started there were three hundred and summat working there, but when I left, I'd say there was about fifty. The Smurfits were Irish, it was a family name. They came to the factory a few times, rolled their sleeves up and mucked in. A real nice family.

Moira Nesbitt on a cruise to Belgium, 1984.

I started courting my husband, John, when I was fourteen, he was fifteen and we married when I was seventeen. He earned good money then, 'cos he was in the brickyard firing the kilns on St Bees Road. Them days, council houses didn't come up quick, but we got the chance of this caravan on the Wastwater Avenue site. Mam was a bit iffy when I asked her if I could get married, but she agreed because we had the chance of the caravan. We had a wedding tea at my mam's with his family and that was it. I married in an ivory satin suit because I thought I could wear that again and I did, soon after. My sister married the following Saturday and I wore the suit to her wedding, too. She got a caravan as well! There were two big sites on Woodhouse, so there were loads of caravans. We waited three years and nine months for a council house and lived briefly on Honister Road in Mirehouse, before transferring to Greenbank to be near all our family.

In Greenbank, everyone was related. We only returned to Mirehouse when Greenbank began to change. All the old people started dying off, new people moving in. We looked out of the window and didn't recognise people anymore; we were always saying, "Who's that?" John kept pigeons and his loft was down on Mirehouse, so it seemed a good idea to get a house here.

When we first moved to Copeland Avenue there were no trees along St. Bees Road; I could look up the hill and see my old house, and could look right down to the harbour from my back step. The council planted trees because the houses used to flood. We were on a hill and the water poured down it in heavy rain. I remember it came down like a waterfall. Over next door's wall, across to ours, over my wall, a river flowing down. It was an inch off my patio window, one time. I was out in my dressing gown, no wellies, water flowing around me to the front of the house, then out, and down to the main road. That's why it was called Mirehouse down here, always flooded at the bottom. Planting the trees made a big difference.

My husband was a top pigeon flyer; he had hundreds of birds. He'd had pigeons since he was fourteen. There were a lot of pigeon clubs then. They used to fly from France. A Federation van came and collected them and shipped them to France. We trained them ourselves. Saturdays on race days we would make flasks of tea and sandwiches and sit and wait for the birds to come back - it only took them eight hours to fly from France. Summer nights when there was a race we would sit at seven or eight o'clock at night waiting for them. You used to see that bird coming and it gave you such a thrill! My husband could recognise all his birds within a flock. Even the last fortnight of his life he wouldn't get rid of the pigeons. He moved bedrooms so he could see out. He'd say, 'Gaa down and let me see you touch that blue 'un lass,' and I'd say, 'Which one? There's ninety-nine of them!'

Moira Nesbitt

Moira and John Nesbitt with some of their prize pigeons.

Moira and John Nesbitt (2003) enjoying some local culture on a trip to visit their daughter, Angela, in South Africa. Angela lived there for thirty-two years before returning home.

Wild Flowers Everywhere

I grew up on the Greenbank estate; the houses there were built in the thirties. A lot of people from the old Newhouses, as they were called, moved up to Greenbank from town. My mam was born in Ingleton, it used to be in Yorkshire then, and her family moved to West Cumbria. I was born in 1945. There were seven of us altogether, but we lost two of my brothers. Patrick died at nine months old in the operating theatre. They used chloroform then and my dad was told they had used too much, but he thought the doctors had done their best, so he didn't take it any further. Desmond was run over by the coal car when he was only three. My dad's hair went white next day after that. My dad was a contractor and he worked on these houses in Mirehouse when they were first being built.

When we were kids, all the lads used to cross the road and come down to the Mirehouse fields to play. It was just meadows here and wild flowers. I remember going over the fences and landing in mires, getting in a right mess. Where our house is now on Newlands Avenue, the water is only a couple of feet down. We got gas in and the gas man laying pipes thought we had a flood. He got a bucket but he couldn't empty the hole out, the water just kept coming back! So the Water Board came out, but they said, 'No, there's no leak anywhere, that's the water level.' Just two feet down! Touch wood, we haven't been flooded yet. There were *so* many wild flowers growing then; I went to Ireland for a month once and when I came back my garden was just full of wild flowers everywhere.

For much of my working life I

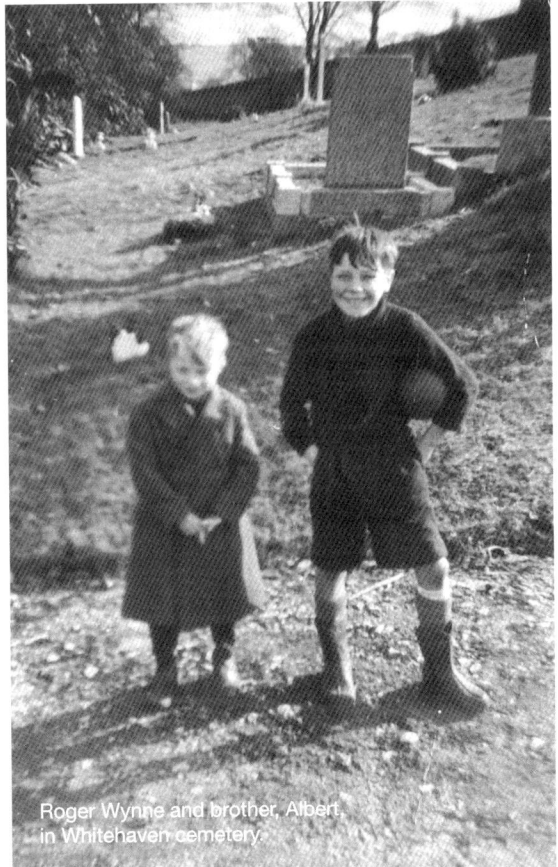

Roger Wynne and brother, Albert, in Whitehaven cemetery.

was up at Haig Pit. I worked there twenty-three years and left in about 1984. It closed soon after; there was coal there still, but there were a lot of faults and you couldn't get it. My first job was the plastic factory in Egremont, they made handbags and pouffes. I was there nine months, then I went to the pits. I couldn't go down the pit till I was sixteen, so I worked on the screens first, sorting the coal. We went to Workington Solway Pit to do our training then came back to Whitehaven Haig. There was some tough lasses on the screens and I took a bit of ribbing on there! Going down the pit, there were some scary moments sometimes, but you got used to it.

I wasn't a union official, but I was on the group who met with management once a fortnight to consult about what was going on in the pit. At Haig, there were strikes in '72 and '74 and both lasted about seven weeks. They were 'All Out'; there were no one day strikes then. They had to run the stockpiles of coal down, so you had to be out for a while. There was no strike pay, but we got some help to feed the family. You had to go down to the Civic Hall and give your details and you got a little bit of money for your dependants, but nothing for yourself. It was hard, but we got a tax rebate, plus miners got cheap coal so we had enough of our own stocks to last a few weeks. That's how we got through.

In 1982, when the president of the NUM, Joe Gormley, retired there were a few miners allowed to go to his retirement dinner in Workington, in the Westlands Hotel, up by the golf course. Everyone who worked in the mine had their tokens put in a draw and that decided who went. Mine was drawn out, it was number ten, and I mind someone saying, 'you don't want that, scopp it back in,' because of No. 10 Downing Street. That's how I got to go to the dinner. We sat with two union officials who looked after the pensions. One of them says, 'You'll regret the day you get Arthur Scargill in,' because that's who was taking over as president. He thought there'd be strikes all the time once Scargill was in charge! Haig Pit closed, so the workers there weren't involved in the big strike of 1984/5.

One of the other big employers here was Marchon. They started off in the early forties making firelighters on Swing Pump Lane, near the multi-story carpark, before they began making detergent at their chemical factory in Kells. I remember, some days there were great lumps of soap suds used to come drifting down from Kells, even as far as Mirehouse. It was as if you'd blown the top of hundreds of bubble baths! Some said it could be really bad through the night, but we never saw that. It smelled really strong. When it came down we used to bring the kids in, and the pram, if the baby was outside, because the pram would get covered in soap suds. In Woodhouse a few people got compensation, because they said they couldn't grow anything in their gardens, but in Mirehouse we just took it as part of life.

After Haig, I went to Sellafield – more money for less work! I got thirty-five pounds a week more. The pits didn't pay well in comparison to Marchon and Sellafield. One of the lads said, 'You must've got paid a lot of money at the pit'. So I showed him my pay cheque and he said 'Getaway!' I went as a contactor first. I was only there a week and then a fella said he needed an assistant in the fabrication shop, so that's where I ended up. When I first went for a job at Sellafield I thought I hadn't got it 'cos the man said he wanted a driver, but I couldn't drive. He said, 'a fella yewer age, yer should be able to drive!' So when I did get offered a job, I took my wages and thought, 'I'll have driving lessons'; I used the extra money for that. I brought home about a hundred pounds a week. The flat money was similar to the pits, it was the bonus that made the difference; it was to stop strikes and the like.

For nights out in Mirehouse there were loads of places to go: there was the Greenbank Club, the Labour Club, the only one still left. There was the Calder Club, St Benedict's Club and the Legion, on the bridge. The Legion was a large hut and they called it the Ponderosa, after the TV Western, because there used to be such a lot of fights. There was a youth club used to be here and that was run by volunteers. One of the men that climbed Everest, I think it was John Hunt, he came to speak at the youth club. There's not much left now.

Roger Wynne

Tradesman's Entrance

In my early years, I was brought up on Bardy Lane on the harbour, where they are building the new flats behind Argos. I lived there with my Grandma, Ruth Gilhooley, my mum and my sister, Ruth. The land there belonged to Grandma. She'd had it about fifty years, but me and Mam moved from there to Bransty when I was eleven. Grandma left the house to my mother, but Mam couldn't afford to repair it to standard, put in a bathroom, a damp course and hot water, so the council gave her some choices. They said my mother must either: knock the house down and keep the land, sell it to them for five pounds, or give it to them and they would give her a council house. Well, we needed somewhere to live so she took the council house and signed all that land over to the council for nothing. Now they're building flats on the land, and it's probably worth a fortune! I still have all the letters about it. In those days you could wait years and years for a council house and we couldn't wait, so we had no choice really.

My grandmother looked after me and my sister, Ruth, while our mother was at work, so I spent a lot of time with her. Grandma was such a character; she was like an early feminist. She was born in 1872, but only married when she was thirty-seven, in 1909. That was late for those days. Before she married, she was a keen cyclist, going with her cousin Willie Watson all over the Lake District. They visited the Isle of Man and Ireland, taking their bikes with them.

It was through her friend, Margaret Knox, that Grandma met her husband. A lot of people went to South Africa then, from this area. Margaret was out there and she asked James Gilhooley to take a letter home to her friend, Ruth. He was a miner working in South Africa, but he didn't like it and had decided to move back to Whitehaven. So, he delivered the letter and that's how he met my grandmother.

Grandma Ruth left school when she was twelve. She did deliveries on her bike for Hudson's Grocers, but she got the sack. One morning, she'd already taken a load of groceries to a house up on Inkerman Terrace, but then the customer had gone back to the shop and asked for a quarter pound of ham, to be delivered! So Ruth had to go back again to the house with the ham. In all her majesty, up she went with it and knocked on the front door! That's why she got sacked; the back door was the tradesman's entrance.

One job Ruth had was selling fish off a handcart. With her sister Isabelle, she ran a bakery out of Hogarth house where they lived. It was at the top of Rosemary Lane, opposite the Mission. Another time, she ran a fish and chip shop out of Bardy Lane, cooking the fish and chips on her coal fire range. Gilhooley's fish and chips. When I was little she still sold bread, and hot cross buns on Good Friday; people used to come and buy them from her house. After the war, she was in her seventies by then,

Ruth Gilhooley and Janet Wynne, aged two, outside their home in Bardy Lane.

Janet Wynne and her pet dog, Flossie. Flossie was devoted to Janet and her sister, Ruth. It followed Ruth to the bus station one day and she ordered it to go back home, but Flossie never returned home and was, sadly, never seen again.

she would bulk buy jam, candles and matches and sell them from her living room.

Grandma Ruth owned a lot of property. She'd bought the Bardy Lane house well before she was married. She bought Hogarth House and the house next door to it, plus she owned a lot of houses around the harbour. They were eventually condemned and had to be pulled down. She was supposed to put fences round her land if she wanted to keep it, but she never did and she lost it. Grandma was a big worker for the Conservative party; she stood once in Harbour Ward for a seat on the council, but never got in. If anyone was in trouble they always came to Ruth. If someone died, they'd come to Ruth for a nightie to lay them out in. She took in her husband's two nephews when their mother died and took in Christina, a neighbour's daughter, when her mother died. So many people seemed to rely on her, but Ruth relied on no-one and worked hard for everything, all her life.

When I was seventeen I married Roger and we lived in a bedsit on High Street for a year. The house was divided up into different living quarters. Getting a council house was wonderful because we didn't have any hot water or a bath at the old house. Everything was washed in the sink by hand and hung in the yard to dry and we shared the toilet with two other families.

In January 1966 Roger and I came to live on Mirehouse and we've lived in the same house on Newlands Avenue ever since. When we moved here our Diane was twenty months old and she said, 'Who lives upstairs?' She'd been so used to sharing a house with other people! We got some furniture given off relatives, as you did then. We didn't even have a tele. We hired one from Relay Rentals about a year later.

The Mirehouse estate was planned originally to house incoming Sellafield workers. The plans show it was intended to be a garden estate with fewer houses and more open spaces. There was to be a senior school on Whinlatter Road, a cinema, allotments, playing fields and a community centre on the green opposite the shops. When houses were built at Seascale, a lot of Sellafield workers preferred to live there instead. That meant the council was able to relocate people here from the town when their homes were demolished.

I spent twenty years raising my family, then I went to work for a company called the Family Supply; later they renamed it Provident. They lent money through a voucher system. You could exchange the voucher for goods in local shops and then you'd pay them back weekly. The interest rate was extortionate, but when you look back now, it was one way people could get credit. I collected for them for eight years and I was pleased to pack it in because I didn't like hounding people who couldn't pay. I kept getting sent back to knock on their doors, but living on Mirehouse, you knew

LAWTON & NAYLOR.
SOLICITORS.

COMMISSIONERS FOR OATHS.

HENRY LAWTON.
HAROLD DAVID NAYLOR.

TELEPHONE No. 392.

St. Nicholas Chambers,
Lowther Street,
Whitehaven.

HN/JM   26th May, 1956.

Dear Mrs. Wells,

                        re 13 Bardy Lane.

        We now enclose the Deed of Conveyance received today from the Corporation in respect of the handing over to the Town of this house and the site of the cottages at the back.

        Please sign this Deed opposite the seal where indicated in the presence of some witness who is then required to sign his or her name and add address and occupation where also indicated. When this has been done please return the Deed to us in the accompanying stamped addressed envelope when we shall of course be retaining it here until such time as we have word from you that the Council have provided you with a Council house as already agreed.

                                    Yours faithfully,

Mrs. E.J. Wells,
13 Bardy Lane,
West Strand,
WHITEHAVEN.

Solicitor's letter to Janet Wynne's mother regarding the transfer of their Bardy Lane. home to the ownership of the local council.

people's circumstances and you didn't want to hound them. One good thing was the job fitted in with looking after the children and I made a lot of friends going round Mirehouse. I shared the customers' joys and sorrows. I got to hear all their news: who had married, who had died, who'd had babies.

For thirty years our neighbours were Reuben and Sheila McAvoy and we could always rely on them if we needed help. There were lots of children living here then; every house had children. People seemed friendlier and you knew everyone along the road. On our street some of the mothers used to sit together on warm days, knitting in each other's gardens while the children played. Sometimes they would take all the children and go off together to St Bees beach for the day, or they might take them all to Wellington beach, a big group of them. People helped each other out a lot: 'Can you pick me up a prescription, if you are going into town?' that sort of thing. We always had a garden full of children, five of our own and their friends. They'd make tents over the washing line, and eat homemade chips in newspaper. If they wanted to go somewhere they would shout through the letter box, 'We're going to such and such.' Mirehouse used to have a carnival every year, the kids loved that. In 1977, for the Queen's Jubilee, we had a street party: tables and chairs down the middle of the road, a wellie throwing competition, dancing in the street. I took part in the rugby match, women versus men!

All my children went to Valley School. I was going back and forth to that school for twenty-six years; I'm proud of my association with the school. Mr Purdham was the Head, then Mr Coan. Some of those teachers taught all my daughters. There were so many children on Mirehouse that the school had to build extra huts for classrooms. The toilets were outside. For heating, they had stoves in the hut with guards round them – it wouldn't be allowed now! Later, there was a community centre attached to the school and a young man to run it, and he set up a Young Wives' Club. We went on outings, had visitors giving talks, but in the nineties it was abandoned because many of the women with children began to go out to work.

A lot of services have gone from Mirehouse. There used to be a clinic on over the bridge, and two midwives lived on Meadow Road, at the bottom of Newlands Avenue, because there were so many home births. There was a doctor's surgery up on Hollins Close. A policeman lived where McColl's shop is now and he would know all the kids. But there was hardly any crime.

In the eighties, before the community centre was built on Seathwaite Avenue, there were Portacabins instead. Iris Templeton ran fundraising bingos and Pie and Pea suppers from there. Newlands Avenue had a butcher's, a grocer's and, at one time, a chip shop. We had loads of mobile shops too. Eric Parkin came with groceries. Thomas Herdman would come twice a week with shovels, paraffin, wood, hardware stuff. I worked for him in town, my first job. You could order in town from Herdman's, something big like a dustbin, or a clothes post, and he would bring it on the van. There was Pip's grocery van at night. There was Handycash groceries, the lemonade car, the fresh fish car. Home and Colonial would deliver, they were in King Street. It was the first supermarket in Whitehaven, around where Dorothy Perkins is now.

In town it was heaving on market day, with loads of young people about, not like now. I would walk into Whitehaven with the Silver Cross pram and could put all the shopping in the bottom. Mother lived at the Ginns by then and I would call in for a cup of tea, or she would walk into town with me. Even the girls had to walk it. We walked to Cleator Moor visiting, or St Bees to go to the beach. You walked everywhere.

In those days, everyone had holidays at the same time; the factories and the pits closed for the same fortnight. We would get what was called a Rover ticket - you could travel on the trains for a week to Morecambe, Blackpool, Keswick had a train line then, Grange-Over-Sands, Windermere. We used to like Barrow because it had a fairground during the holidays and a park for the girls to play in. You'd come back late at night and then you'd have to make sandwiches ready to be off again next morning. We used to go with our friends James and Josephine Mason; they had five children, as well. There were good buses then, running till late, so you could get home alright. A lot of people went to Butlin's in Ayr during the works fortnight. Coachloads used to go up, but we were married over ten years before we had a proper holiday, and then it was to Blackpool.

Janet Wynne

My Link Road Lake

Opposite my house is a lovely copse,
In summer it's bright and green.
The trees there softly sway,
In the gentle summer breeze.

In winter, when there's a lot of rain,
We get a village pond,
I call it Link Road Lake,
And of it, I'm very fond.

When it's frosty and it freezes,
It's like a skating rink,
The children come around to play
On our little lake called Link.

Seagulls think they're ducks
As they swim on Link Road Lake,
And from my window, they *do* look like ducks,
But I know they are just fake.

Then after winter, it drains away
And soaks into the ground,
We get our little green copse back
When summer comes around.

Jenny Doran

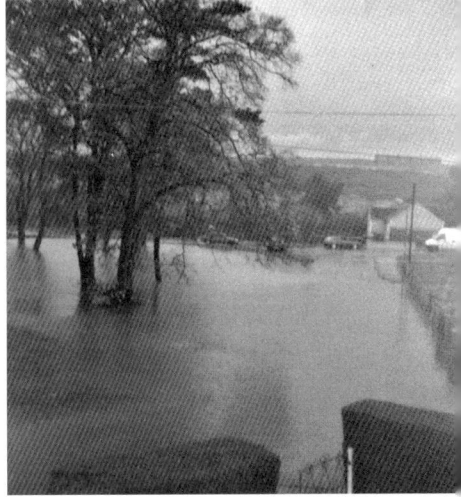

Above: Flooding in Link Road, photo
courtesy of Jenny Doran.

Below: Mirehouse Ponds, photo
courtesy of Jenny Doran.

The Calder Club

The Calder Club was the place to go
The people of Mirehouse loved it so
Groups came from far and wide
Artists, singers, comedians, you were lucky to get inside.
People booked it for weddings, christening parties too
And some for funeral parties, which sadly wasn't a 'do'.
There was a lovely lounge, where people gathered for drinks and chat,
Men played cards and dominoes, while the women talked and sat.
There was badmington and bingo, a quiet snug to sit and browse,
To sit in peace and quiet, away from all the crowds.
At Christmas there were parties, one for children too,
New Year's Eve was a great night out, we were often there till two.
It was the best club in Cumbria and sadly now it's gone,
But we will never forget the Calder Club,
For in our memories
It lives on.

Jenny Doran

Sink or Swim

Joe Wells (stage name, Hank), husband of Betty Wells.

My name before I was married was Elizabeth Gibson, that's my posh name, but I always got Betty. My mam was Bette. Like Bette Davis. In 1966, I was living in Paisley and I went on holiday with family and friends to Butlin's holiday camp in Ayr. They always had entertainment there. Well, this young man came on in the talent contest and sang *Old Shep.* He had a lovely blue jacket on with red insets, I remember, and looked very smart. The redcoat introduced us after, and we got talking, but it was almost the end of the week and the holiday was nearly over. He asked if I would have my photo taken with him, so I went into the Beachcomber hut and we had one taken together. That was the end of August and he won the heat at Butlin's, so he had to go to Ayr again for the finals. We met at Ayr station and we went to the camp together for the day.

Betty and Joe Wells meeting in Butlin's, Ayr (1966). Right, Betty's friend, Irene Boyd.

We corresponded after that and by Christmas we were engaged, then married the following July! I was courted by letter! His name was Joseph Wells but he went under the stage name Hank Wells; he was a country and western singer in the clubs. Joe lived in Woodhouse, in Whitehaven, and he had gone on holiday on his own to Ayr because a friend had let him down.

When we married I moved to Whitehaven. It was very difficult to get a house in Scotland, but here it was easier. So we lived in with Joe's mam and dad for about nine months and then got this house in Lorton Close in 1968, and I have lived here since then. The whole area has changed now; there wasn't any fencing at that time, it was all open plan. On Seathwaite, where the Community Centre is, it was all houses, but they pulled those down. They kept flooding because

A blossoming romance: Joe and Betty Wells courting, Cold Fell 1967.

this is a bad area for water; it's marshland really. They should never have built here, because when it rains the gardens get flooded, but they were always first to flood at Seathwaite. There was nothing to be afraid of in Mirehouse, the children could play out and there was nothing to harm them.

Before I came, I didn't even know Whitehaven existed. It was very strange at first, coming here, but it was very, very friendly. When I came the first time it was to meet Joe's mam and dad. I was twenty-three years of age and I had never travelled in a train by myself! I was always with my family. Joe met me in Carlisle and we came through to Whitehaven and got on the top deck of the Woodhouse bus and everyone was talking at once and I thought, 'What have I done? I've come to a foreign country!' I couldn't understand a word, it was so Cumbrian. Fortunately, I could understand his mam and dad, and his sister. But there was this friend of Joe's! We would all go out after we were married, six couples, and the friend would be telling jokes. I would just nod and smile, but I couldn't understand anything he said!

I started work in St Bees' School for a year when our two boys, John and Alan, were grown up a wee bit. I worked in the kitchens and I got three shillings and sixpence an hour chopping vegetables. After that, I went to work in Woolworths and I worked there for twenty-six years. I loved it. It was so busy, lots of staff - we even had stockroom boys - and it was good fun interacting with all the customers. We sold everything: we had a great haberdashery counter, biscuit counters, vegetables and groceries. We sold paint and had a lovely kitchen centre, so it was entirely different. But when they renovated, all these departments were cut down to a really small amount. It was their downfall.

They did look after their staff at Woolworths. We used to get a bonus at Christmas, but that stopped. At twenty-one years' service you got a party and a gift to choose. They were really good. We used to go to Workington to dance, the staff dance. We used to have a canteen as well, with proper dinners. There was a cook. It didn't cost much and there was a lovely Christmas dinner. They did away with that gradually: the cook retired and we had just a microwave.

I ended up in children's clothing and then went on the till. I liked it. Elderly customers would come in and you got to know them. Sometimes you were the only person they spoke to all day. Just saying, 'How are you today?' made a difference. There was one old bloke used to drag me over the counter for a kiss. I always had red lipstick on. They called me hot lips! One of the under managers, I gave him a kiss on the cheek once. No one told him he had great big red lips on his cheek and he walked round the shop all day like that!

Another time, I got offered a king size bed! We had such a laugh. I served this elderly gentleman one day and I said, 'Have you got any money?'

He said, 'Aye, lass, you'll want for nothing with me. I've even got a king size bed!'

Isabelle, my friend, looked at me, and then at him, and said, 'You'll be dead within the week!'

'Aye,' says he, 'but I would die with a smile on my face!'

We had a lot of fun, but it came in that you hadn't to call people 'Darling' or 'Pet'. Nowadays, you can't say anything. One old man when I said, 'how are you today, Pet?' I thought he was going to hit me; he went ballistic shouting, 'Don't call me an animal, I'm not an animal!'

Two ladies I knew well were stood there and they were shocked. Next thing, Tony the Irish manager came along and said to me, 'Hello Pet!' Some customers could be nasty, but most of them were absolutely lovely, more of them were lovely than nasty.

I was going round tidying in children's clothing one day when I spied these two well-dressed gentleman carrying a big box. I said, 'Can I help yer?'

'No, we're awright thank you,' they said. So they went.

Five minutes later the boss came up – big, tall fella, all legs. 'Oh, I've had a call,' says he, 'We're to be on the lookout for two gentlemen with a big box.'

'They've been and gone,' says I.

'What!' He was like Basil Fawlty jumping around. He said they'd been pinching clothes and shoving them in the false bottom of the box. He went running up King Street with his big, long legs flying, little me running behind, and him shouting, 'Can you see them?' Well, I wouldn't have known them again if they stood next to me, unless they still had the box! Whether they actually got anything, I don't know.

Another time, I stopped a fight. There was a big scuffle: two fellas were rolling around on the ground. They were fighting over a girlfriend. Me, the size I am, there's nothing to me, but I jumped in between them and said, 'You two, if you want to fight you'll have to come through me first!'

So that was Woollies, never a dull moment.

For nights out in Mirehouse there were all the clubs, which were thriving, and most people from Mirehouse went to one of those. At weekends they would put on entertainment, mostly singing. Joe did all the clubs around here. He carried on with his music after we were married. He was well known: he'd been on television, *Cock O'the Border,* before we were married and I went to Border Studios with him for that. He was a real good singer.

Joe worked at the Electric Board, then Jackson's timber yard, and finally at Sellafield for a year as a security guard. He was paid off and he never worked again after that. Joe became ill; he got Huntingdon's disease. He would be about fifty-four when he got diagnosed, but it had been there a long, long time before that. We had a fight to get invalidity benefit - that was quite a story. He got sick money and then went on to invalidity. He was sent to doctors in Workington twice and they decided he was fit for work and we had to appeal, but they stopped his money anyway. We had no income for six weeks, just the bit I earned. It was horrendous. I was trying to cope with him not being well, not knowing what was wrong, trying to work, and then had to go to a tribunal in Carlisle. You're in a room with all these people judging you, trying to catch you out. At that time he was having trouble even walking in a straight line, I had to help him on with his coat, and he was having some fits. The questions they asked, it was so degrading, but fortunately they classed him as unable to work.

They say about care in the home, but they are cutting down on that. Luckily, I'd a good care package, but I only got it for the last three years of his life. Carers came in two, or three times a day, then four, to do his personal care. The boys were here and that made such a great difference to me. I couldn't have done it without them; it meant there was always someone who could be with Joe. I went to West Cumbria Carers and it was great: to be able to go out and get away for the day and talk to people really helped me. There is help there, but it's knowing how to get it. Life! It's like trying to swim the Channel: sometimes you go under but, luckily, I always managed to get back to the surface!

Betty Wells

It All Went In The Purse

I was born Kathleen Davis. I'm from Dublin and my family lived just off O'Connell Street. Because we lived in the inner city, we weren't allowed to play out on the streets as children, so we'd go every day to Mountjoy Square Park, where they ran loads of activities for the kids: crafts, sport, Irish dancing and things like that. We'd have a great time and I was happy there.

A lot of my relatives died when I was young. When I was twelve, my mother went into hospital with a spot on the lung. She was in hospital eight months when my father died suddenly in the night, from a haemorrhage. He came in from work, had his tea and went to bed at seven-thirty. Then he woke up at half-past one being violently sick. He called for my sister, May, to send for a priest but he died before the priest arrived. My older sister was seventeen then, but there were another five of us younger than her, so my mother signed herself out of hospital and I left school. I went before the school board and they agreed I could leave, so I that could stay home to help Mother. She wasn't fit and, at thirteen, I took over the household. Even eighteen seems to be still a child these days, but you had to just get on with things then.

Three years later, Mam died. She'd no other treatment after leaving the hospital, so she never recovered. In Dublin, you had to pay to see doctors, so you never really bothered with them much. She took bad one Tuesday night and when the priest came he arranged for her to go into hospital. I didn't see her again after that. The last thing she said was, 'Take care of each other,' and we did. When she died, there were two sisters younger than me; the youngest was ten. Both of them were terrified they would be taken into care,

Mary Davis, mother of Kath McLean.
Joe Davis, father of Kath McLean.

but no one bothered us. We just carried on by ourselves.

'The purse' was there sat in the cupboard. The older ones went to work and gave their wages to me and it all went in the purse. Everything was written down that had to be paid out of it. Because she knew she was really sick, Mother helped us get organised like that. She knew we weren't going to get help from anywhere else when she was gone; there were no social services to look after you, you were on your own. But you didn't feel sorry for yourself. Only now and again, if I was washing all the clothes by hand, or had a sink full of dishes, I might do, but very rare.

At seventeen I got a job. it was thought it'd be better if I got a job, so as to meet people my own age. I went to Palm Grove ice cream factory and from there I went to Lemon's Pure Sweets. I was there a couple of years, then I went to a makeup factory, Max Factor – all the good names! I moved on again from there. It was always my own choice; you could take your pick of jobs, if you got fed up. I didn't realise how flitty I was. I worked in umpteen places, but there were so many jobs to be had.

I've been over here forty-eight years. I met my husband, Leo, in Mosney Holiday Camp, near Dublin. It was a kind of Butlins, and later it became an asylum centre for refugees. We met in the Pig and Whistle bar on the site. We were married in Ireland in 1967 and there was a lot said about marrying a protestant. But I said, 'I'd rather be married to a good protestant than a bad catholic!', so the priest got dispensation and we were married without too much trouble. We had a do in a hotel and then night time everyone came to the flat. It was in the city centre and those town house flats were very big, with huge high ceilings, all fancy cornices. The floor shook all night with the dancing.

Leo's mother lived on Windermere Road in Woodhouse and for about nine months, we lived with her and then got a flat of our own. We had trouble understanding each other for a bit, myself and Leonard's family: I'd be washing the 'delft', not the dishes, and putting things in the 'press', not the cupboard - and then there was the Cumbrian accent to contend with! But I've never regretted coming, I've had a good life here. I was amazed that in England they offered you free milk when your children were born! And there was the NHS! There was none of that in Ireland. You only got your family allowance once a month in Ireland; I got as much in a week here as you'd get in a month there. People thought I was rich - the family back in Ireland thought I'd done very well and landed on my feet coming here. Even now in Ireland you have to pay a lot to visit the doctor. I was born in 1942 and, though Ireland was neutral in the war, there were still ration books. It was a struggle to feed my brother and get him proper help growing up, because he was a coeliac. My dad had to make a special box to sieve his food.

The flat Leo and I moved into was on the top floor and it was such a struggle up and down the stairs. One of my children, Peter, was born there; I didn't make it to the hospital! I thought I had another month to go, but I wasn't feeling well and knocked on my neighbour Shirley's door. She ran and got my mother-in-law

Above: Kath McLean and Leo in 1970 with their revamped Mini. Their sons, David and Peter, are in the picture. Their daughter, Jennifer, was born two weeks after this was taken.

and called for a nurse, but Peter didn't hang about and he was born before the nurse came. What a commotion: there was me in the bed with Peter, and the cord still to be cut, my David on the floor, Shirley and her child, the nurse, my mother-in-law! The ambulance men carried me down the stairs in a hammock with Peter wrapped up in fresh nappies and me calling 'Oh, mind me bottom!' because the hammock was sagging over the stairs.

In the flat I'd to bump two children and the pram down the stairs first, leaving one at the top, screaming at the gate till I got back up. I'd to walk into town, 'cos you couldn't get a pram on the bus, then all the way back up that steep hill with the shopping and the kids. I admit when we lived in the flat we looked down over Mirehouse and the whole valley was black, thick with smoke. Everyone had coal fires then. I used to think, 'I don't want a house down there!' But it we were offered a nice house and it was better than struggling with the stairs in the flat. We moved to Lorton Close in 1970 and we've been here happily ever since.

Moving to Whitehaven, to be honest, it was all a bit of whirl: marriage, setting up house, children. I did get homesick, but we got a car and could drive to Liverpool to get the boat across for visits. The car was like a mini-van, a beat-up old thing with no back seat, so Leo had to put one in. It was dirt cheap; he paid one hundred pounds to buy it, do it up and put it on the road. It was great and at weekends we'd go off to Keswick and Ambleside, somewhere like that, so Leo could show me all the sights. When the children went to school I started driving lessons. Leo had fractured his arm and couldn't drive the car for months. He'd tried to teach me to drive for four years, but he'd take me down little lanes near St Bees and away into the country - it was terrible! You'd think he didn't want me to pass my test! After four years it was a joke at the Labour Club that the L plates were painted onto the car.

Anyway, I went and had proper lessons and then I ended up volunteering for Meals on Wheels and driving a van. I did that for a good while, till someone said to me, 'Why don't you do this and get paid for it? Go on the Home Help.' So I did, for seven years. On two occasions I found my clients dead when I arrived! It was a shock, but I wasn't frightened, or disturbed by it. Growing up in Ireland, you are exposed to death from an early age, going to wakes, seeing the dead, so I was OK about it. Being a Home Help then, it wasn't the same job as it is today. You'd to do everything: we cleaned windows, hoovered, ironed - real housework, whatever needed done. If someone was ill, you'd take their washing home and do it yourself, pick them up a bit of shopping, so you did much more than your paid hours. But it was your own choice. You were happy to help people, if they needed it.

Kath McLean

Right: Jennifer, David and Peter McLean wearing hand knitted sweaters made by their mother. Kath learned to knit when she was only four or five years old.

Vimto and a Straw

I was born Anne Hartley in 1939 and lived in No.15 Sandhills Lane, Whitehaven, opposite where the old fire station was. The house is gone now. We had a cellar. It was dark as anything. The gas meter was down there and Mam used to say, 'Go down and put this shilling in.' I was terrified! It was a creepy old spot. They tried modernising them houses, but in the end pulled them all down.

Because the house was condemned, when my sister, that died, caught TB, we got the new house on Dent Road, Mirehouse. It had four bedrooms and two toilets: one upstairs and one outside! In the lanes, we just had the one outside with bits of old newspaper for toilet roll.

All the kids played out in gangs about the town. We used to go into the top of Castle Park and slide down the hill on lumps of cardboard. We'd go in the wood and make bows and arrows and all be Robin Hood, or we'd go to the Golden Sands on the harbour and pretend we were in Hawaii. At the castle, above Wellington beach, we were Knights of the Round Table. There were a lot of people living in the town then. The houses up by Mount Pleasant, well, we thought we had nowt, but you wouldn't believe the conditions people lived in up there: piled one on top of the other, shared toilets. God love them.

We went to Quay Street School on the dock. Behind Argos there's an old church and the school was attached to that. At dinner time, we had to come out of school and walk over to Howgill Street, whatever the weather! There was a canteen there during war, the Utility Canteen, and all the schools used to go there. You'd have one school line of Catholics coming this way, Protestants going t' other way and kids used to shout across the road at each other, 'Proddy dogs', or 'Catalogues'.

Father died early, in his thirties to forties, of coronary thrombosis. I was about eight or nine when he died. Mam had five kids, so she had to go out to work - cleaning offices, delivering papers, that kind of thing. Where the pet store is now at the bottom of Preston Street in Whitehaven, there was a caravan used to come and a fella used to kill chickens on the spot; the women would all come along and pluck them. That was one job Mam had. She worked hard to keep us fed; sometimes she took us to the shore, picking cuvens to eat. We went to William Beach to pick coal that was washed up, as well, but we had to be careful not to pick slate, or it would spit back out of the fire.

When the war was on, there was barbed wire all over the beach. It was maybe because of what happened in the First World War when a German submarine came up and shelled a chemical factory in Lowca. The story goes, everybody came running down to Whitehaven pier to have a look at it and watch what was going on, instead of running away in case they were shot! One tragedy I remember is the day St Nicholas's church burned down in Whitehaven town centre, in 1971. I was in town and the bus had to stop because the smoke was so thick the driver couldn't see. A woman ran up and was hammering on the bus door, desperate for the driver to let her in because she was choking and couldn't breathe.

Like I said, our Betty died when she was young. She'd been an usherette in the Empire picture house. I had a brother, Ted, he was next to Betty, and a sister, Lynne. She joined the army and moved to Cyprus. She was in the army when the Suez crisis was on. She went to South Africa after that to make her fortune with her mate, not that the fortune ever appeared!

When we were growing up Mam used to go every week to Blencathra Nursing Home in Grange, near Keswick, to see my sister. We used to look after each other while she was gone. Betty was in there twelve months and had one lung removed. She came home and we had a party for her birthday - well someone made some cakes! She died on December thirteenth 1951; she was only twenty-one years old. It was King George's birthday the day she died, and strangely, he died on her birthday a few months later, on February sixth 1952. We all had to go to the clinic and get patches stuck on and injections and orange juice, so the rest of us didn't catch TB.

Coronation time, 1953, I was thirteen. My other and various neighbours organised all these events to make money for the kids. We had a Mirehouse carnival. I didn't know what I was going to go dressed as, but Mother got me in a swimming costume, threw a towel over my shoulder and labelled me 'Miss Mirehouse'. My brother Billy, she had him with a jacket on, and a straw hat, his arms lifted up and stritched out with an auld brush shank through them and straw sticking out the ends. Mother's fundraising took local kids on La'al Ratty for a train ride; we had a street party and a day out at Blackpool as well!

Mirehouse Carnival Committee, Third from the right is Anne Chambers' mum, Mary Hartley. Second from the right, Mrs Finlay. Mrs Wigham is second from the left.

Mother would brew her own beer and when they had committee meetings the beer would come out. She would sell it for sixpence a pint. I remember the smell of it still. Mrs Crosby, Mrs Skillen, Mrs Wigham, they would've been on the organising committee with my mother, and Mrs Quayle. Some of the lasses from the other streets came down and asked to join our party on Dent Road, but there were a lot of different parties going on all round the estate.

We used to climb trees at the bottom of Dent Road. Before the Calder Club was there, there was an old hut where workmen went in to have their bait and we used to go in there. We'd practise to have a concert; we were always going to have a concert and never did. We used to tap dance and sing: a lass went dancing at Cowper's School of Dance and she would come and show us what to do.

When I left school I got a job at Edgard's; I made cuffs on the coats. People made different bits: someone might be on sleeves or other bits of the coats. I can't remember if I got one pound and ten shillings, or two pound and ten shillings a week. Mam gave me ten shillings pocket money out of that. I had to buy my own dinners at Peeney's; a plate of chips, a slice of bread and butter a cup of tea was a shilling. I bought cigarettes out of that as well and maybe kept a shilling to go dancing at the Empress. The Rhythm Aces played there, like a Glenn Miller Band. The frocks with big petticoats came into fashion with Rock and Roll, but they would itch the legs off you. Sometimes we used to go to a cafe called Higham's beside the Queen's cinema and get a bottle of Vimto to share between half a dozen of us with a straw. The woman used to come over and say, 'If you're not buying anything, out yer go!'

At seventeen, I got a job in Sellafield in the canteen. Mother had already got a job up there, a decent job, she really earned. I was a day worker and I got seven pounds a week, much more than at Edgard's. I went out on a mobile van round the site selling tea to the contractors. The contractors would give you all this blarney to chat you up. That's how I met my first husband, a lad called Bill Quinn, from Ireland: he was giving me the blarney, then I met him again somewhere in town and he asked us t' go out. The town was heaving with contractors at the time, some of them were teetotal but they would all go down for a night out.

Anne Chambers performing at a fundraising Hawaiian night.

Anne Chambers performing at St. Benedict's Club. Jim Clark on drums.

I married Bill when I was twenty and we lived with my mother, while we waited about five years for a house. But in 1968 we decided we would emigrate to South Africa - HMS Windsor we went on. The kids were only tots, two of them, and we emigrated in the March, got there in April and by July my husband was dead. July the seventeenth. They said it was coronary thrombosis. He'd got a job in a gold mine and I remember that last day he went to work: he opened the door turned round and looked at me, went out, came back in and looked at me again. I said, 'Tarrah,' and that was it. Next day, they told me he was dead. I was twenty-nine, he was thirty-six.

So, me and the kids had to turn round and come back home. We came back and lived with Mother on Dent Road and I went to work at Quaker Oats at the harbour. Chopper bikes were the fashion for the kids, so I worked twelve weeks on night shift and earned enough to buy the kids a bike. I was packing sachets of instant porridge into the boxes. Seasonal work. Then it closed down and I went to Smith's paper mill on the north shore. About twenty years I worked there till Mother died, I was fifty-three. There were three deaths all close together in my family then and I felt I'd had enough. I just threw in the job.

I met my second husband George at St. Benedict's Club. I used to sing in there and up at Kells Legion. I sometimes put on charity concerts, so I guess the childhood practice paid off in the end! Hank Wells would come and play for us. What a lovely man he was. I'd sing anything – Frank Sinatra to John Lennon. My brother, Billy, was musical, as well, and he was bass player in a group called Billy and the Rebel Men. When he died in 1986 there wasn't a soul in Mirehouse that wasn't touched by loss that day. The church was chock-a-block, there were people out on the green, the whole community came and the paper wrote up an article about him…about the day the music died.

Anne Chambers

WHITEHAVEN NEWS, WEDNESDAY, MARCH 26

HUNDREDS AT FUNERAL OF POPULAR RU COACH

More than 500 mourners from the local Rugby Union and music world attended last Friday's funeral of St. Benedict's RUFC trainer Billy Hartley.

Mr Hartley, 44-year-old father of four, collapsed and died at a club training session.

St. Benedict's RC Church, Mirehouse, was packed to overflowing, and hundreds stood outside.

Fr David Murphy, parish priest, officiated, assisted by Fr John Watson.

In addition to his rugger interests Mr Hartley had his own music group.

He worked for 17 years at the Marchon Works, Whitehaven, where he was a storeman, and whose management were represented at the funeral. It was followed by interment at Whitehaven Cemetery.

News cutting reporting on the funeral of Anne Chambers' brother, Billy Hartley. Reproduced, with thanks, courtesy of The Whitehaven News.

An Empty House on Greenbank

My maiden name was Pritt and I was brought up on Bransty, where I was born in 1932. There were five of us, three girls and two boys. My eldest brother is still living and he is ninety-four now. My brothers, my dad and husband, all of them were miners, at one time or another. One brother left and went into the Navy, one went into the Merchant Navy, and Dad went to work in a munitions factory in London for a while during the war. That left me and two sisters at home with Mam. We lived on North Road, which was quiet and pleasant, and there was never any trouble. I loved my mother a lot, but Dad was not very nice to her and they didn't get on; I wonder if that's why he went to London. But Mam took him back. I felt sorry for her; she had nothing.

There were a lot of rows at home, so my childhood was not always pleasant, but there were happy times too, and we walked round here on Mirehouse in the lovely fields every Sunday, before all the houses were built. We wore charity clothes from school, but everybody had hard times then and we were no different to anybody else. Even when my husband was working it was hard; you'd be 'ticking' from Monday to Friday 'cos the kids came first – food, school clothes, anything like that. I'd get groceries off the van on tick. I was frightened of debt, so I didn't get a lot and I'd pay it off every Friday. Danny was in the pit thirty-four years, but he didn't get a good wage and, early on, there was hardly any overtime. He used to grab it when he could.

When I was young, a group of us lads and lasses used to go to the pictures together; there were different picture houses you could go to and this lad, Danny, said to his friend, 'I'm going to whichever one Edith's going to.' So we all went to the Queen's and I was walking home and Danny caught up with me. We were walking up Bransty Hill, you know how steep that is, and he said, 'How far up do you live?'

I said, 'Only half way.' I've often thought, if I'd live at the top, it might've been the end of the romance! He had to walk all the way back to Kells after that, down one hill and up another!

I was two and half years older than Danny and he had to ask his dad's permission to marry me, because he was only nineteen when we married in 1954. In our early marriage we lived in five places: with my mother-in-law in Mid Street, Kells, with Danny's sister next door to that, then my sister's in Lorton Close, Mirehouse, then to my mother's, and then Greenbank! I was happy with my mother and we should never have left there. I thought Danny didn't like it, but I found out too late that I was wrong about that. I left her, and I regretted it.

We ended up living in with this old woman on Greenbank. It was terrible. We had one daughter by then. She was three, or four. This old woman, she'd fell and hurt her head, so her son-in-law and daughter took her in to live with them. This fella, he said, 'Listen Danny, there's an empty house on Greenbank. Mother-in-law is gonna live with us, so why don't yer move in.' So we did it out a little bit, not a lot, and bought a bedroom suite on tick and moved in one Saturday.

Well, on Sunday we were sitting and a car drew up. Danny's sister was with us and she said, 'There's a car outside with a bed on top - it's the auld woman!' He'd brought her back! I was so mad! He'd one eye and I felt like putting t'other one out. I had two years of misery after.

I felt sorry for the old lady because she'd had a hard life and I tried to be nice to her. I made her meals, cooked her Sunday dinner on the old, black lead fire. But I couldn't do owt right. One day the back boiler bust behind the fire grate, there was water running everywhere, and she blamed me for it! It'd been in twenty-five years! 'Look what you've done now!' she said. Danny was on the teatime shift, six at night till two in the morning, and she used to wake me up and say, 'Danny's knocking,' but there was no sign of him, 'cos it was only one o'clock! I used to be so tired.

When I got the letter to say I'd got this house in Coalgrove Road, it was such a relief. When we left, we left a coalhouse full of coal and took nothing except our bedroom suite - it as all we had. But I heard some of her family had said we'd taken all the light bulbs! One day, Danny was going up the hill to Kells and she was coming down t' the house and she stopped him and said, 'I didn't like 'er Danny; I liked you, but not 'er.'

The day we moved to Coalgrove Road, I was ecstatic. The only table we had was a tiny bamboo coffee table off my mother. We bought a new suite - on tick again! Danny's mother bought all our curtains and that was all we had. We had no money, but we were happy. We'd walk to St Bees, or Wellington beach for a day out. Once I won seventy pounds at the Bingo. It was about 1962, so it was worth a lot then. We were going to Edinburgh Zoo the next day with the three kids and it meant we could afford to go to a cafe in Edinburgh and didn't have to take sandwiches. What a great day we had! I won the money at the Empire. It was falling to bits by then; the floorboards were rotten and mice were running around. I remember sitting there like this, with my legs up on the seat shouting, 'It's a mouse! A mouse!'

A couple with a baby lived in this house before we moved in. It was a Sellafield house then and the woman here had a chip pan fire and tried to run outside with the burning pan, but poor lass, it blew back all over her and she got badly burned by the fat. So they moved out, it was a real shame. A terrible thing, but so easy done.

I've never regretted moving here. The neighbours were all lovely. A lot of the people on the street have lived here as long as me, or longer. We talked to everybody; we knew everybody and talked over the fences. People were pleased to get these houses and looked after them. What we didn't have, we didn't miss. We were happy as long as we had each other and the kids were fine, and they all were.

Next door, our first neighbour, Ned Templeton, he died when he was forty-two. My husband loved him; he was a great man. He was like a Pied Piper. We'd go all round the fields with him and the kids, collect conkers, take a bat and a ball and play games with them all. He used to say, 'Come on, we're going swimming and he'd walk all the kids off the row into town and take them to the baths. 'Yer don't need bus money,' he'd say, 'you're all walking it!'

For a bit of fun, I used to play darts. Me and Danny practised together and went into competitions round the local pubs. Certain competitions we played doubles and I played with the lasses on the women's teams. I'd learned darts after we were married. Danny bought me these darts, they were great big heavy things; when they hit the board it was thud, thud, thud. A fella said, 'Did you used to be a knife thrower in the circus!' But I used to do alright with them. We had a great life but nothing that cost a lot of money.

I worked at Smith's before I married, their spot on the docks, packing tea bags. My first job was at Eugene's in the market hall, making rollers for perms. The market hall was a wreck: we'd go upstairs and half the stairs were rotten, with boards missing. After a bit, they moved from there to a new factory at Hensingham and we had a

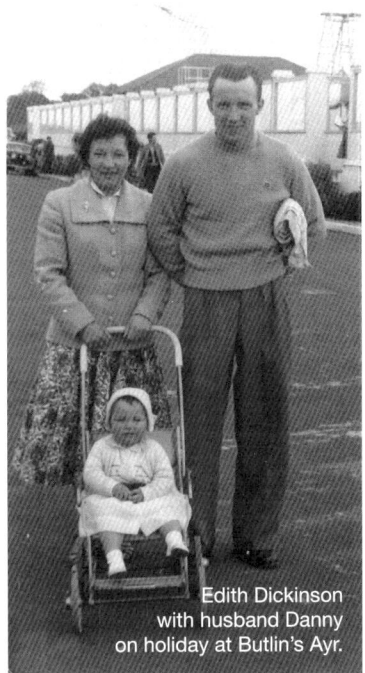

Edith Dickinson with husband Danny on holiday at Butlin's Ayr.

Fun and Laughter on Coalgrove Road. Left, Peter Dickinson. Centre, John Templeton. Right, George Dickinson.

Edith Dickinson with her children and mother-in-law on Mid Street Kells.

Staff at Eugene's Factory 1952. Front row left, Edith Dickinson. Second row, far right, is Kitty Shimmin and next to her is Olive Stone. Back right, Doris Farrer. Photo courtesy of Edith Dickinson.

1956, Young Wives group performing a tribute to the 'Tiller Girls' in Whitehaven's Castle Park. Funds raised went to Cheshire Homes. Photo courtesy of Edith Dickinson.

big banquet - Lord Adams was there. His niece was our boss. We were opposite Sekers, fire station side. I was a machinist at Edgard's for about nine years after I was married. That's how we could get things for the house, carpet and that.

Menzies newsagent's was on Queen Street, and I was a cleaner there for a lot of years. That's where they sorted the newspapers for delivery all round Whitehaven. After five years, they moved to Lillyhall and I said I couldn't get there anymore. But they said they'd take me in the delivery van! So the driver would pick me up and take me all over the place delivering papers. Then he'd drop me at work and bring me back home again when I finished cleaning. They were good to me there: if I was off work sick, which was very rare, they used to mark me in and pay me.

My last son was born ten years after the others. I had a bad time, in labour for two days, but he was worth it. All the children were home births. It was commonplace to have them at home and mostly it was great. A midwife came for all of mine; she lived just a few doors away from here and did the home births on the estate. Gary started at home on Saturday night, but wouldn't come. The midwife was with me all time and she phoned the hospital on Sunday night, but they wouldn't take us in. I was being sick and was dehydrated, so Monday morning she phoned up and insisted they took me in t' the hospital. I had him half past ten on Monday night - if he'd been the first, there wouldn't have been any more!

Gary was vacuum extraction and they covered his head when they gave him to me because it had such a big bump on it. Then I never seen him for a fortnight, they took care of him. They kept me in hospital all that time. I'd splints on both arms, because I'd had all sorts of tubes and transfusions. They brought me a big plate of dinner after he was born. I was totally famished, but I couldn't eat it 'cos I couldn't bend my arms for tubes! The nurse came along and she whipped the plate from right in front of me and saying, 'Not hungry?' and away she went!

When I was working in Menzies in town, that's when my husband died. He was fifty-two. It was 1987, May the eighteenth. It was tragic – a brain haemorrhage. Billy loved swimming. We went to the swimming baths every Sunday with a friend up the road. When we came back we'd make dinner together, but he said this day, 'I've such a headache,' and went to bed. He was there all afternoon. I went up and shook him and he didn't open his eyes, but he talked to me normal, so I thought he was alright. But I got more and more uneasy. I kept going up and he still had the headache and I thought this isn't right. So when I went back again and I couldn't wake him, I came running down stairs two at a time saying, 'There's something sadly wrong with your dad, George, get the doctor!'

I had such a horrible feeling. It was like everything had stood still and I was trapped inside a bad dream. The doctor came and he seemed to move so slowly - I wanted him to run! The doctor said it was a slight stroke, but it wasn't. We went to hospital and stayed with him all night and he died next day; he never gained consciousness. We were so close; we did everything together. He was such a good husband. I tried

Paintings produced by Edith Dickinson at her Age UK art class

lots of things to fill up the time after he died, like sewing and quilt making. Now I do oil painting. I go to classes at Age UK every week and my family think I'm getting quite good!

Danny always wanted to go abroad, but I was terrified of flying. We flew once to Jersey and everyone said, 'Get a good stiff drink inside yer and you'll be alright.' But by time they gave out the drinks we were landing, so I had t' knock back my gin and tonic and get off! When the pit closed and he got made redundant, Danny persuaded me to go with friends to Marjorca. We got on the plane and it started lifting and then went 'bang!', so we taxied back to the runway and they fiddled about with the engine for about two hours, with us all just sat there in the plane! It was terrible; I never loosened my seat belt the whole time, and then it took off again! He loved that holiday, swimming in the sun. The next year we were going to go to Minorca and we were looking forward to it, but he said to my daughter he didn't think he was going to make it. We thought he was worried about his dad, who was ill. Danny never complained, but maybe he wasn't feeling well. We were counting the weeks till we went, but he died just a week before. I was so disappointed for him. Whenever I go on holiday now, I think of him and how he would have loved it.

Edith Dickinson

Taking Root

My family name was Wylie and I was born in Whitehaven in 1928. My family lived in Mark Lane where Mark House was, up a little passage called Woods Court. There were three houses up the passageway. There was me, two brothers, Grandma, Mam and Dad that lived in the town house. The lads had the top attic. We had paraffin lamps, no electric and no bath. We paid to go to the slipper bath once a week, where the swimming pool was, and we could always have a swim off the Golden Sands as a way of getting bathed!

When you think about it we just wandered on t' the beach and round the town; Mother never thought about it. We went about in groups and had a lot of freedom. We weren't frightened of anything, but we were told to behave ourselves, or else! We just kept together, played about, looked after each other and came home when we were hungry. When we moved up to Kirkstone Road, I wouldn't let the children out unless I was with them.

In 1950 my mother got this house on Kirkstone because our old home was condemned. Me and Wilf moved with her because she was a widow. The old house was seven shillings a week, but this one was one pound and nine pence and Mother said, 'However will we afford that!' Wages were nothing compared to what they get today. I worked for peanuts really.

I worked in the Market Place Post Office for a Miss Reynolds and I got two pounds a week wages. There were three sisters, none of them married, and the elder two had the Post Office in the market. I worked partly in the Post Office and partly in the house and they used t' give me a dinner. That was my first job. They were lovely, lovely people. They were reserved, nice, quiet people, and I enjoyed them. Then, when they gave the Post Office up, they moved up to Sneckyeat and I used to go up there to see them. When I had our Ann, I used to go up with her and they idolised the child. They left me some money when they died and, to me, it was a godsend. They were really kind. I couldn't believe it when I got the solicitor's letter to tell me they'd left me something.

Mother couldn't get over it when we moved into Kirkstone Road. There was this tiny little fireplace and Mam said, 'We can't cook on that!' I was working at the time and I would come in and say, 'Mam, put the light on!' because she wouldn't use the electric light. The paraffin lamp in the old house was far more dangerous, but she was afraid of the electric. I said, 'Mam, it won't harm yer.'

There was no road when we moved. No buses. No Hollins Close, just rough track. Yewbarrow Close wasn't there. The Bethshan Care Home was a farm and we went there for eggs and potatoes. There was Hollins Nursing Home; the building is the Water Board now. After operations you'd be sent there for a fortnight to recover. Wilf went over and talked to his brother through the fence when he was in there after his op. We're the only people to live in this house since it was built sixty-five years ago. People ask why I don't move 'cos of all these steps outside and I say, 'I'll move when they come for me with a box!' I'm quite happy and I've got a good neighbour.

Mind, I've had lots of neighbours. When we moved here it was Sellafield house, council house, Sellafield house, all the way up the road. People were coming because they were giving them a house with the job. All strangers. They came from further afield; Barrow a lot of them came from. They were all kind, but to me, they were strangers. When the Sellafield people moved out into private houses, then their houses were given back t' the council.

I can't believe how the years have gone by. Dad was a miner in William Pit. He'd a cousin, James McMullen, killed there. The pits were everything; most people I knew worked there. We all ran across the Wagon Road to the pit head when William Pit exploded in 1947. It was really frightening when they fetched the men up. James drove some of the machinery down there and the gas got him. He was just sitting there upright, but dead. There was a lot of crying women on the pit top; everyone had relatives down there, so it affected a lot of people. There were many people wore black around the town for a good while after. Mother shopped in the Co-op so we went there and all got black hats to mourn our cousin. He was young, twenty-seven, had two children, a handsome lad.

Living on the harbour, there were always coal wagons going by. For some reason, a bolt would come out of the wagon sometimes and someone would shout, 'Wagon bottom dropped!' Like lightening everyone would run out with a bucket and take off with all the coal. It was gone in minutes. It was only years later I realised it wasn't an accident that the bolts came out!

Dad retired from the pit at fifty-five through ill health and went and worked on the railway. He always said he'd been gassed in the war and had trouble getting his breath. He loved going fishing. We would say, 'Well, we know what we're having for tea!' We would take a flask of tea down to him and he would say, 'Sssh.' He would sit for hours; we'd sit there for a bit, then think, 'this is boring,' and we'd be up and away somewhere to play. We had many a fish dinner.

The pits, that's all there was; these days it's Sellafield taken the place. There was fishing, a lot of fishing boats. When we moved up here to Mirehouse, there was a man called Oscar lived on Honister and he was on the boats. His wife would bring us fish and say, 'Here, Oscar's been fishing.' People were kind; they gave all the time, not wanting anything in return because we were all in the same boat.

Mother used to go to the washing baths in Strand Street on Mondays. She put all the dirty clothes in a basket and on our way to school we used to carry the basket to the baths. We'd pick it up when we finished at four, all washed and dried. There were big dryers there: you dragged the pulleys out, loaded up and shoved them in to dry. It took Mam all day. Dinner time, we'd come home and make her a sandwich and take it up to her. She'd be scrubbing, boiling, dolly blueing the wash. When we got a new house we bought a washing machine and Mam said, 'That washing can't be very clean!' because it had only taken an hour to do what took her all day. She couldn't get over it.

When I got married I thought, 'I wonder what Wilf likes to eat.' I loved Mother's broth; she used to make it a great pan of it and it would last for days. So I made Wilf some of that. He said, 'Well, that was very nice, Alice, but I don't want it again for a long time!' He would eat anything, I used to think he must have no sense of taste, but he wouldn't eat my broth.

I'm not ashamed to say, when I was married I was always waiting for my husband's pay. I couldn't have gone past the Friday. He was a bricklayer by trade, but when we had children he was rained off, frosted off and we'd have no wages coming in, so he went on the buses as a conductor. He got paid Friday and, if he was back shift, he'd go down in the morning for his wages because people came and wanted paid: insurance man, bread man, they all wanted paid on Friday. People don't know they're born these days; they'll spend in a night what I had to live on for a week.

My husband wasn't paid much, but he used t' tip it up. He liked to go for a pint on Friday night, so he got pocket money back. When I first worked I thought, 'What am I going to do with all this? Should I give it to me mam?', because my dad always did. But she said, 'Have you got your wages?' So I gave her all of it. I never smoked. With the money she gave me back I bought sweets, went to the dance and saved something to buy my own clothes. I'd bus fares to pay when we moved here, but the sisters gave me an extra couple of shillings to meet the cost: you'd never meet people as kind as them.

I met my husband at the Empress Ballroom. I couldn't wear makeup till I went outside of the house, so I used to go into the cloakroom at the Empress and put on a bit of lipstick and powder, then scrub it off before I went back home. Mother would've thought I was a Jezebel; she was very strict. There were dances at Kells Welfare Hall and I went there alternate weeks. My aunty lived on Kells and Mam wouldn't let me walk home after, so I had to stop with her. I thought, 'I'll never get a boyfriend to take me home, if I've to stop at my aunty's.' But I did, in the end, and Wilf and I were married fifty-one years. We married in 1950 and people were still on rations. My brother was abroad so he sent us dried fruit to make the cake and friends and neighbours all saved their sugar and butter rations for us to use. A lady called Mrs Craddock made the cake.

Mother thought drink was terrible. Wilf used to sing at charity concerts and often went to pubs to do that when I was engaged to him. He'd say, 'We can't go out because I'm on a charity concert tonight, but you could come with me.'

Mam would say, 'In a pub!'

He'd say, 'She'll only have a lemonade!' and I would, and it lasted me all night.

Wilf's family lived on George Street in town; the house they lived in is still there. Wilf's mother married twice, so had two families and about eight children, not uncommon those days. They were all like steps and stairs, not much between them. Wilf's dad wasn't a nice man. Women in those days, you know, got bashed about a lot. I said to Wilf's mam, 'Why did you stop with him?', and she said, 'I had all these children, where would I have gone?' He had money. Nobody owned a house years ago, but he owned his own. There was a baker's up on Rosemary Lonning that belonged t' him and his sister. Money must have been in the family.

My elder brother emigrated to Australia when it was only ten pounds to go. He wanted to get out of the pits, but you either had t' be in the pit, or the army. He felt trapped, so that's why he went. I said 'You won't go, now Dad's died?'

But Mam said, 'If he wants to go, let him,' and she never saw him again.

In later life, Wilf worked at Leyland's in Distington, making buses. I was always fetched up t' think about tomorrow, but when he got redundancy money, Wilf said, 'It's money we didn't have. We're going to Australia to see David.' I'm so pleased we did that, because David's since died. He had a wander lust, David. My dad's family were a bit like that. I had an uncle and an aunty in Canada and one aunty in New Zealand. But me, I wouldn't move from 'A' to 'B'; I've taken root.

Alice Lindsay

Alice and Wilf Lindsay.

God's Country

God's country, that's what I call Mirehouse. If I try to think of why I feel like that about it, I guess it's because of the strong sense of family and connectedness it gave me. Dad has thirteen brothers and sisters and Mam has twelve and a lot of them live on Mirehouse. As a child, I made friends with all my cousins' friends as well, so the circle of people I knew was massive.

I was born on Derwentwater Road in 1972, so I'm not among that first generation of people to move on to the estate. My maiden name was McLoughlin and my family originate from Greenbank and Woodhouse. Mam was thirty-three when she had me, which was classed as old to have a baby, in those days!

My Grandma was Joan Cunningham; she'd been a screen lass and she talked often about the sense of community she had on that job. Grandma lived right behind us on Borrowdale. My aunty lived behind us as well. Gran started out on Woodhouse, then went to Uldale Road, then to Borrowdale, where she died. It was easy to change houses then. You'd say to someone, 'Do you want to swap?' and sort it out between yourselves. I suppose you had to let the council know at some point, but there never seemed to be a problem. Where we lived, next door had a garage and we needed one so we just swapped. I went to school one day and came out of our house and went home to the house next door! We just had to move our stuff over the wall.

Grandma's house was the big meeting place; she always had a houseful of sons, daughters, grandchildren, cousins, everyone! In later years Grandma needed a lot of looking after, but there was always someone in the house to see to her. People would be coming and going, not in any organised way, but she was never left without help. Sunday afternoon we would all go in and play cards for pennies. I remember one time our family all went on holiday together to Butlin's. There were thirty, or forty of us and we filled a whole coach! Wherever I went, I felt surrounded by family as a child and that makes you feel very safe.

The summers seemed longer and warmer then; the summer evenings lasted forever. It was light till eleven o'clock and we played in each other's houses and gardens till late. Families made a bread bag full of chips and would feed whoever was there. The doors were all unlocked, you just came and went and parents always had an idea where to find their kids.

I went to St Gregory's School and my sister Gillian used to drop me off sometimes, if Mam couldn't. One morning she didn't see me inside the gates, so when she left I just walked all the way home again. Mam couldn't believe it when I turned up because I was just nursery age. I got a roasting back at school from the sister. Some nuns still taught at the school then. The Head there was Sister Rose and she was legendary – very strict and stern. It was a disciplined school, clear boundaries; everything was black or white and the kids seemed to thrive on that. On hot days we came outside and did our work on the grass in the sun.

I always remember the big bonfire we had on the green every year. That was a community occasion -potatoes were thrown in the bottom of the fire for everyone to eat! As soon as the schools went back in September, we would start collecting, going round the doors asking people for rubbish; by November those bonfires were colossal! The police came a few times because they wanted to check there was no-one inside before we set them alight. Kids sometimes made dens inside in the weeks before bonfire night.

We all went to St Benedict's Church. There were several services a day on Sundays with maybe three or four hundred people at mass. Good Friday, Midnight Mass and Christmas Day, there was standing room only at the back of the church. These days there's one service on Saturday, with about fifty attending.

St Benedict's Social Club was the place our family went for entertainment. My brother played rugby for the team and so did all his friends. My aunt, Ruby Dunn, was on the committee there. I would go over to Grandma's about half-five New Year's Eve 'cos Mam and Dad had to queue for tickets for the evening, it was so popular. They would take sandwiches and drinks to have in the queue while they waited. We used to have Easter bonnet parades there, family weddings, and my brother and sister had their eighteenth and twenty-first birthday parties at the club. All the big events in your life took place in that club. My father-in-law is a musician and he played concerts at St. Ben's. He's a living legend, lead singer in Lenny and the Silhouettes and they are going strong. Lenny's seventy-five, still doing charity shows. At a reunion in the Marchon Club a few years ago, you couldn't get a ticket for love, nor money

Dom Pater and his wife Kath were the stewards at St Benedict's Club, but after Dom died on holiday in Spain, there was a line of short term stewards that followed. They didn't put their heart and soul into it like he did. It went into decline, got shabby and slipped into disrepair

At one time, people didn't go out much in town; nightlife was centred on the estate. But that began to change. When I started going out, the White House, on the harbour was the in place to go. When England was playing football, it was heaving. One of the big attractions there was the huge TV screen covering a whole wall. What was funny about going there was that people still sat together according to what estate they were off. Different estates sat in different corners: Kells here, Mirehouse there, and so on. You'd go over and have a crack with someone from another estate, but go back to your own corner. The old swimming baths became a night club, the Park. They boarded over the pool and made a dance floor on top. If you weren't in by half past seven on Saturday you weren't going to get in at all. Your nights were determined by pub opening times. Now people don't go out till eleven, but Whitehaven's dead in comparison to then.

Mam was a nurse; she did her nurse training in Workington (about 10 miles from Mirehouse), but she got homesick! She had to come home again because it was too far from away! She got a job at the old hospital in Whitehaven which was haunted by the ghost of the Grey Lady. She never saw the ghost, but my Grandma was a cleaner at the hospital and she saw her going up the stairs. The ghost never harmed anyone, she was a just hovering figure. The hospital used to be the home of the Lowthers and people said she was some kind of servant from those days who couldn't bear to leave! Mam enjoyed it at the old hospital and thought it was a very supportive place to work. Matron was God. Mam's love of the job must have rubbed off on us, because both me and my sister ended up in nursing.

Dad worked in Haig Pit since he left school. He got sick of working underground, it was a dangerous job, but he worried more about his job security. He got a fair few injuries working there: he had all his teeth knocked out. This chain broke loose, swung at him and knocked them out. A lot of pit men had trouble with their knees and he had a cartilage operation; he came out of hospital when we'd just had a big fall of snow and fell a cropper. He was in agony. In those days you still got cash wages and he sometimes was paid a big bonus. We thought we were the richest family in the world 'cos dad had a fifty pound note in his pay packet once; we passed it all round the family to have a look at it! It was a worrying time when the pit closed, but I don't think Dad was out of work long. He bought our council house with his redundancy money for next to nothing.

I remember when Punk fashion came to Mirehouse! It was the late seventies, or early eighties. On the estate there were quite a few bad lads who used to go around with big Mohican hairstyles with safety pins in their ears, Doc Martens up to their knees. They'd openly walk around the estate glue sniffing - that was a change here, drugs entering the picture. They were really scary. I saw them making petrol bombs, pouring petrol in bottles, putting rags in. I don't know that they ever used them for anything; they were doing it for effect, I reckon. There'd be or three or four in a gang and a few different gangs. I think the older generation were intimidated by that, but it was just a passing phase. The pond became a bit of a no-go area for a while: it was full of shopping trolleys and there were drunks down there. But it's got tidied up and is respectable again now.

1986 was the year of the big snow. It was so deep you couldn't see where the pavement was. Everybody rallied round checking on elderly neighbours, digging out each other's drives. Dad worried about his pigeons; people walked all the way home from Sellafield; you had to put people up if they were stuck with you when the snow came down. A fella with a tractor came down our road to clear it and we all mucked in and looked after each other.

I didn't leave home till I was twenty-eight and I don't know how I managed to drive away, even then. I came down to the middle of the stairs, I walked back up again, came down again. Dad's a quiet man, a man of few words, and he said, 'It's alright lass, if it doesn't work out, you can always come back.' I burst into tears at that, I was in a heap. It broke my heart to walk out the door.

Berny Robson

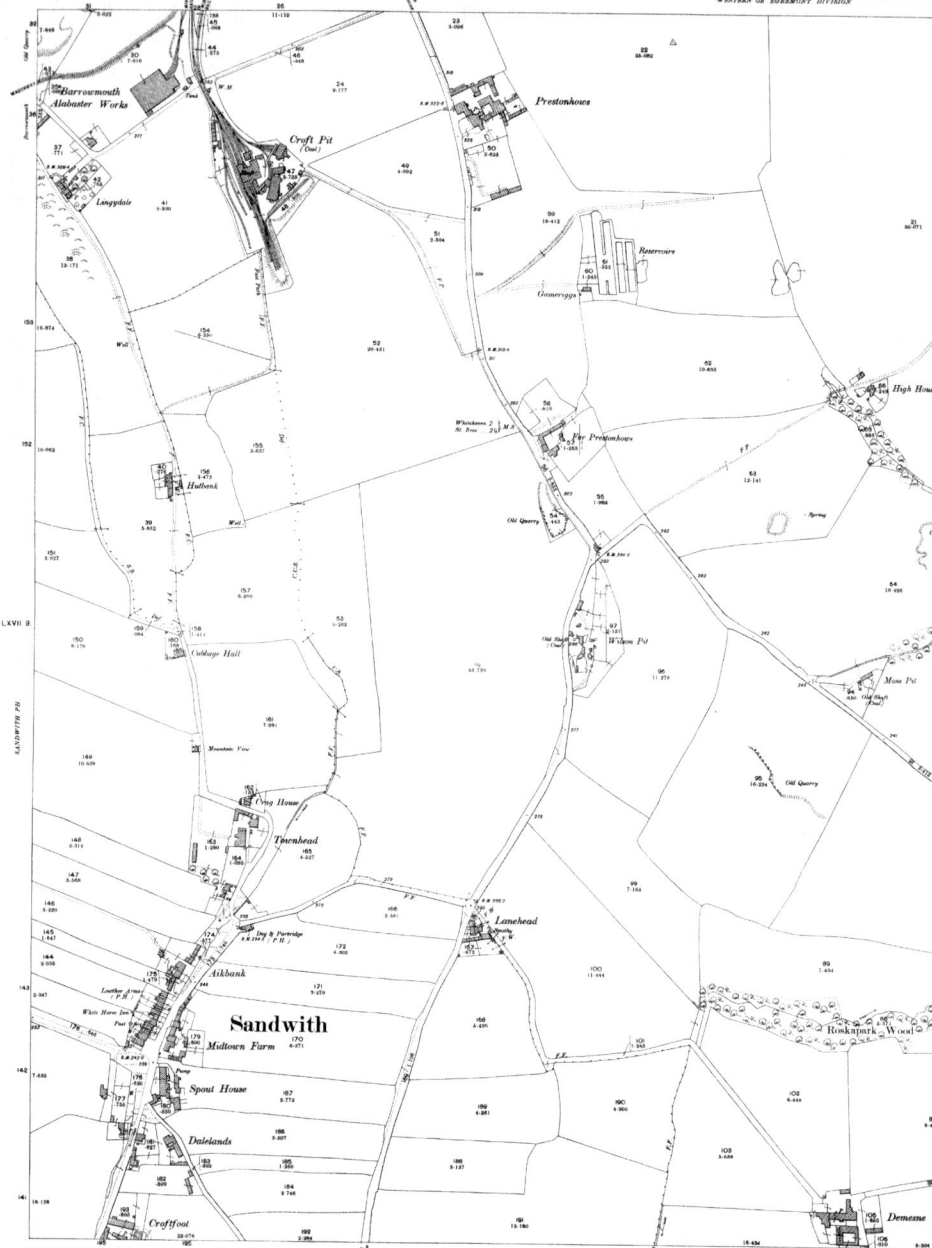

The top right hand corner shows the area later developed into the Mirehouse, Woodhouse and Greenbank housing estates

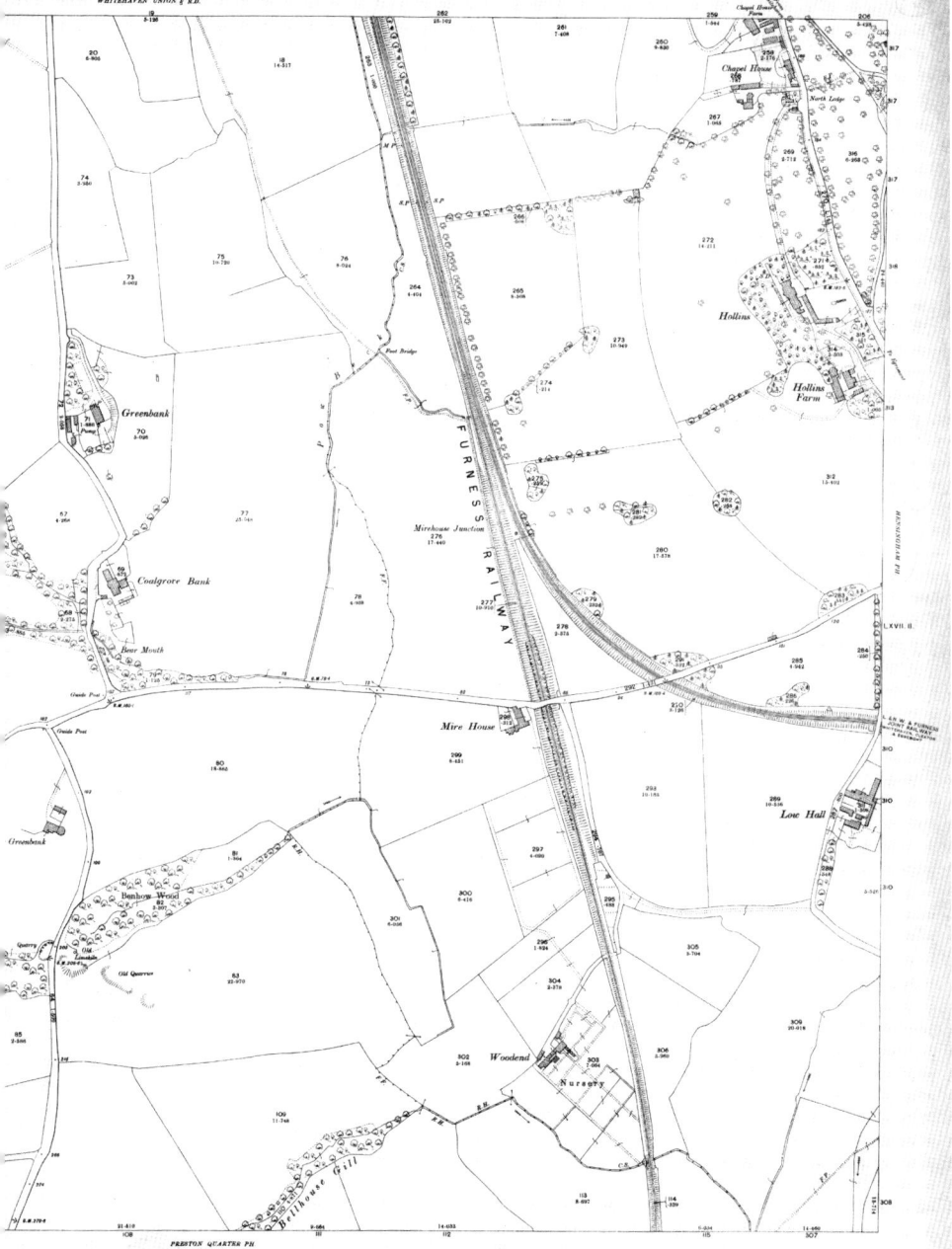

OS map from 1899, reproduced here courtesy of Cumbria County Council Archives.

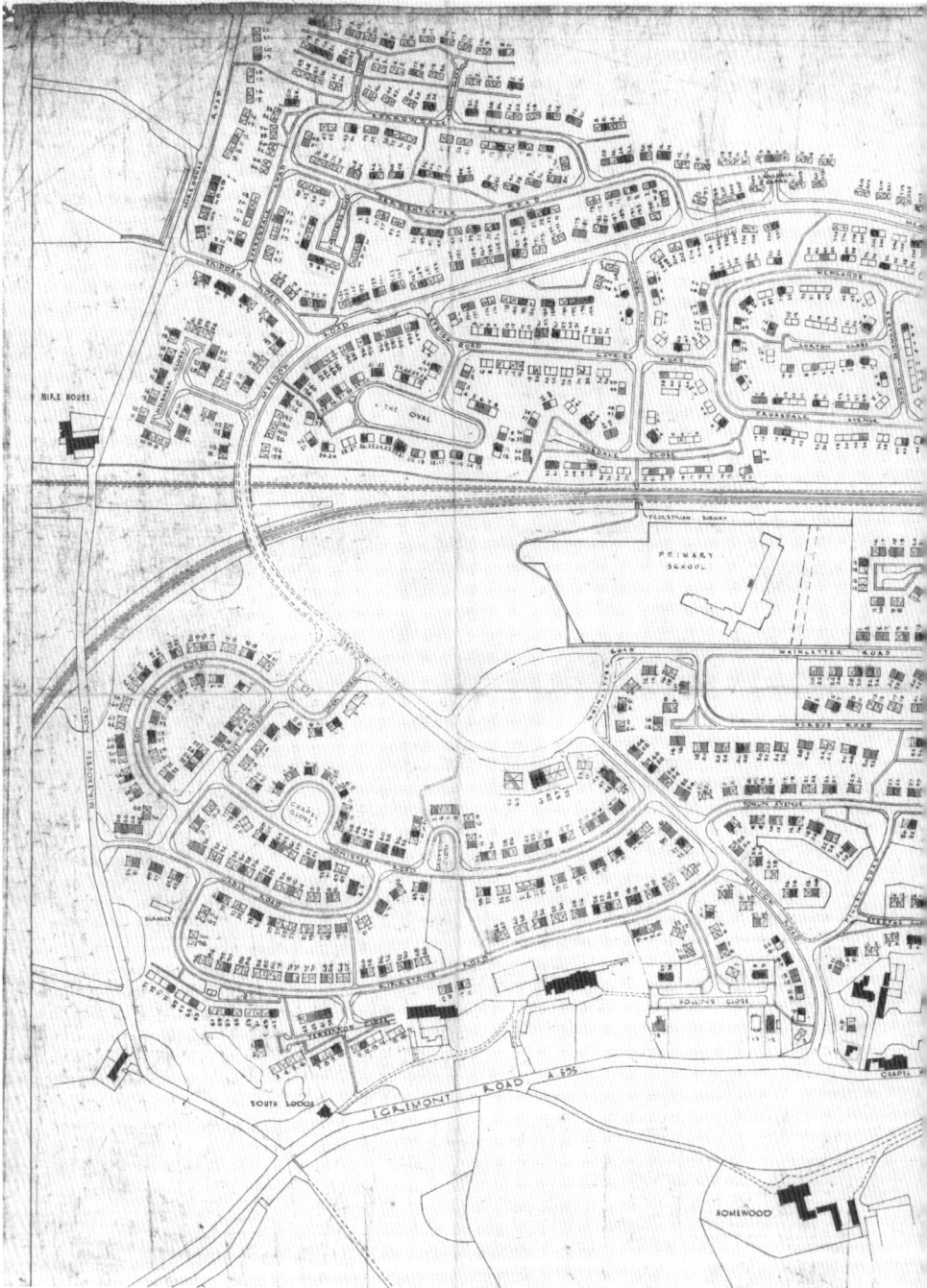

The 1949 street plan for the proposed estate. The upper portion shows the '09' side, Mirehouse West. Top right, Meadow View Institution, was the Workhouse, and Infirmary. The lower portion of the plan shows the '06' side, Mirehouse East.

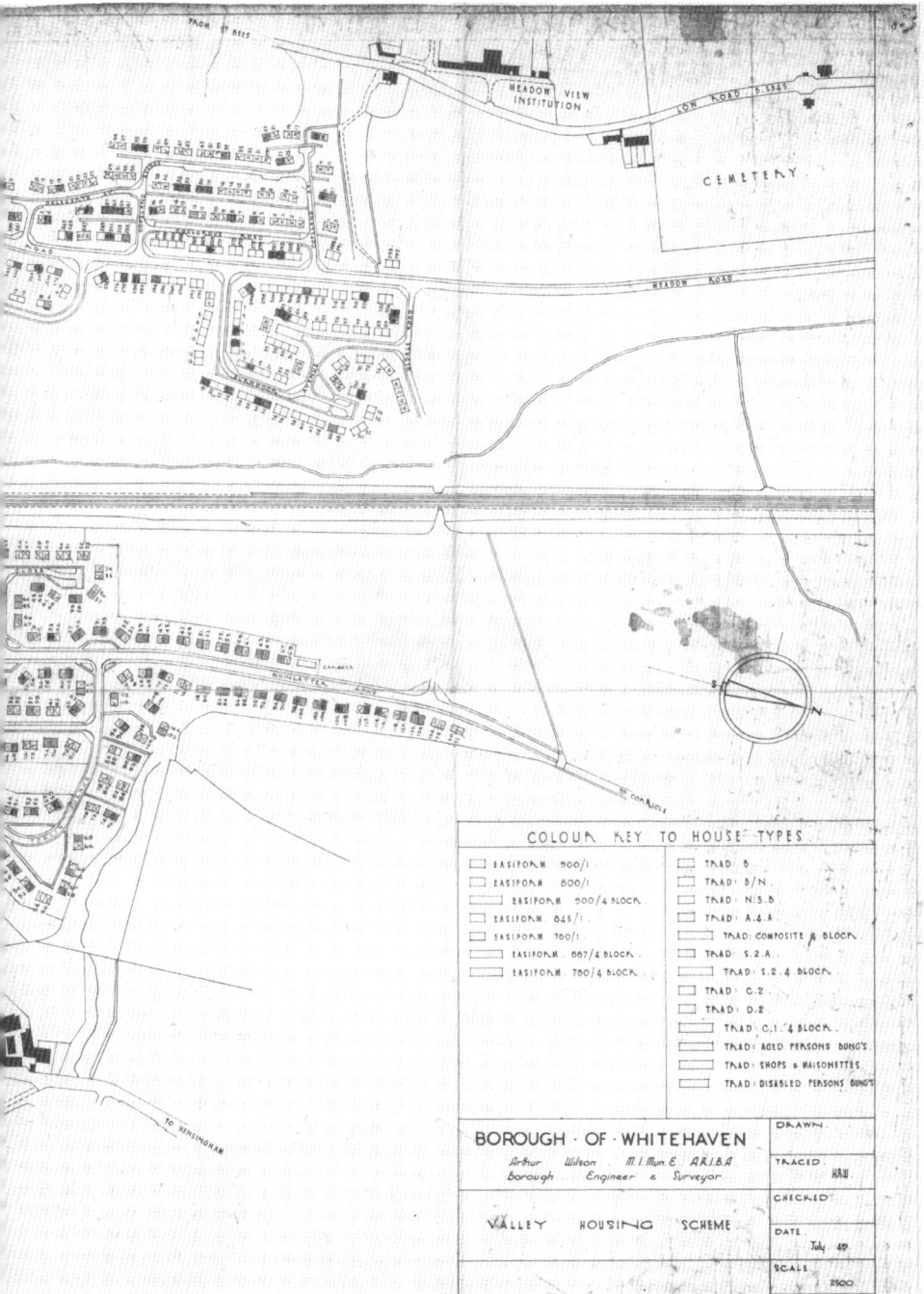

COLOUR KEY TO HOUSE TYPES.

EASIFORM 500/1	TRAD B
EASIFORM 600/1	TRAD B/N
EASIFORM 500/4 BLOCK	TRAD N.5.B
EASIFORM 645/1	TRAD A.4.A
EASIFORM 760/1	TRAD COMPOSITE 4 BLOCK
EASIFORM 667/4 BLOCK	TRAD S.2.A
EASIFORM 760/4 BLOCK	TRAD S.2 4 BLOCK
	TRAD C.2
	TRAD D.2
	TRAD C.1 4 BLOCK
	TRAD AGED PERSONS BUNG'S
	TRAD SHOPS & MAISONETTES
	TRAD DISABLED PERSONS BUNG'S

BOROUGH · OF · WHITEHAVEN

Arthur Wilson . M.I.Mun.E . A.R.I.B.A
Borough Engineer & Surveyor

VALLEY HOUSING SCHEME

DRAWN.

TRACED: HAW

CHECKED:

DATE. July 49

SCALE 1:2500

The shops, school and churches were developed on the '06' side of the estate.
The plan is reproduced courtesy of Cumbria County Council Archives
and Copeland Borough Council

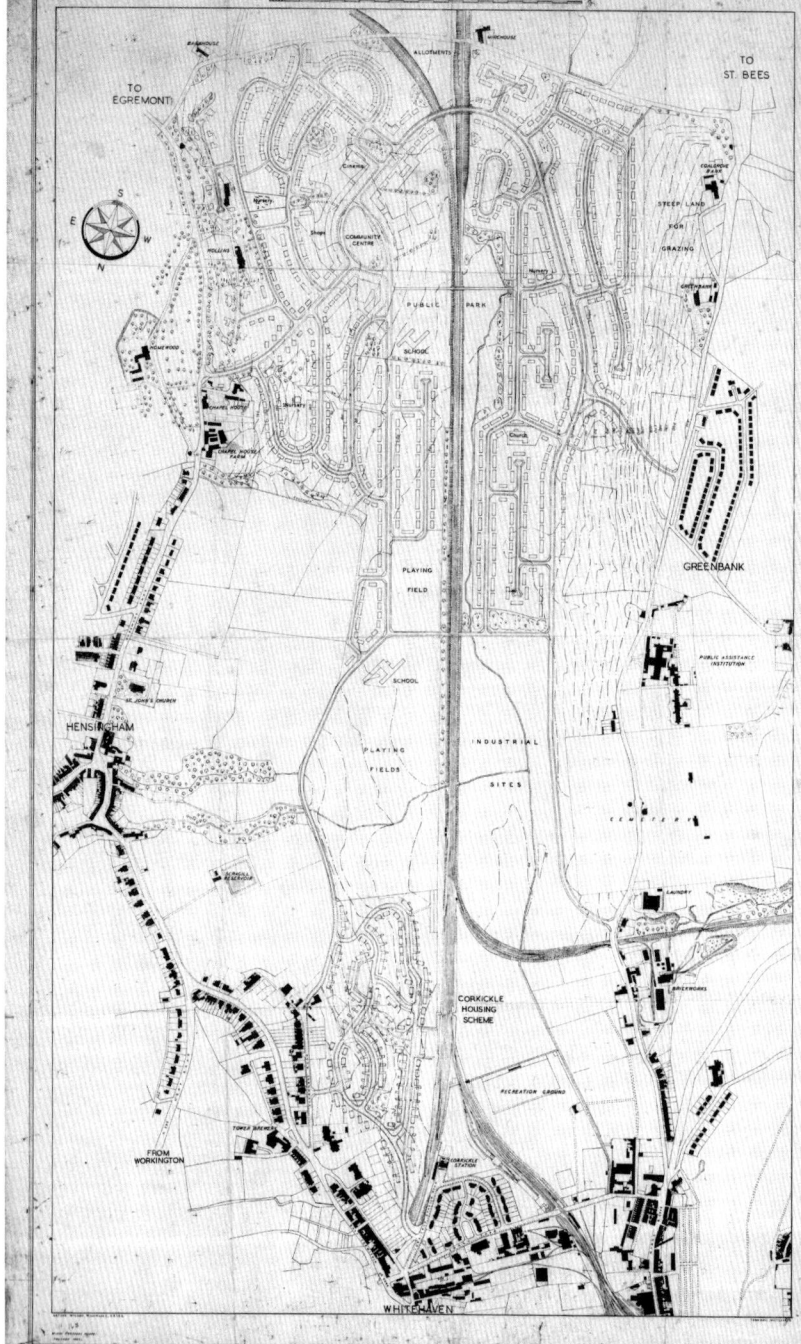

Proposed plan for Mirehouse estate development, reproduced courtesy of Cumbria County Council Archives and Copeland Borough Council. The estate was developed with fewer facilities than appear on the plan e.g. no cinema was included in the final build.